Find Your Why and Fly

"My wife signed up for John's coaching academy last year, and I can't believe how much more focused and confident she is about MLM. I was the classic man trained to work hard in a regular job being Just Above Broke. I decided to come to Florida and have personal training from John to see if this business venture was really going to free me from 40 years of working slavery. After a Level 2 Boot Camp and 3 days of personal coaching, I couldn't wait to get back to the UK to start walking the path of freedom. I believe that when we as students of life cry out for a teacher, one is sent to us. We certainly feel that John and his team have been sent to us. I can now begin to welcome myself back home again this time as a person with dignity rather than as a worker shackled to a treadmill. Bless you John and the team for your Millionaire mission."

- Robert Jenkinson, Business Owner

"After 27 years of study and practice in the field of personal development, I have discovered one shining truth that makes all the difference. You will succeed at any endeavor if your "Why" is strong enough! I've known John Di Lemme for over two years, and he is an absolute master at helping people just like you get what they want out of life."

- Ron Henley
www.RonHenley.com

The Ultimate Success Factor

"John Di Lemme is a must hear speaker for this hour. His story of success and significance is encouraging and life-changing and will remove any excuse from your vocabulary. The wealth of wisdom and knowledge coming from his new book will change your life from poverty to prosperity, from broke to blessed, and from failure to success."

- Rob Yanok, Pastor & Motivational Speaker
www.RobertYanok.com

"John Di Lemme is the real deal! In less than two years after meeting John and implementing his Find Your Why teachings, my life has been totally transformed and my personal and professional dreams have now become my reality. Sometimes I have to pinch myself to ensure it's not a dream. Thanks for being you John!"

- Tom Beal, Founder
www.MLM-Experts.com

"John helped me break through the illusion of the glass ceiling, find my passion, form a plan, and go for it! I've learned to enjoy the journey, and since I'm doing what I love, life is now fun. Thanks John!"

- Mary Andrews, Entrepreneur

"Concept of Find Your Why: My Why is at the core of my heart and soul and spirit ....beyond the mind. Yet it gains momentum toward achieving it by filtering it through the mind to be expressed in words for the vision of the future. I attracted a strategic business coach into my life after writing down on paper my desire to have a great business coach for my Network Marketing Business. His name is John Di Lemme. It is a relationship based on a mastermind partnership, coach/student, the Champion within all of us and the "play to win the game" of success attitude. John is a coach that guides me with strength and confidence versus demands with power. My part is to COMMIT to fully follow the process and play the game to win even when the possible seems impossible. John has an amazing amount of knowledge and proven experience that he is willing to share through his coaching if one is willing to step up to the plate . I have done that and at times it is an uncomfortable process. John has assessed my specific needs to get me from A (now) to B (where MY WHY will be achieved). Accountability, integrity and respect are a given in this business relationship. I have learned to trust myself and trust the process. I am learning about leadership by being coached by an outstanding one. My trust in John Di lemme as my coach was there from the first meeting."

- Beverley Johnston, Business Owner

The Ultimate Success Factor

"I met John Di Lemme through a friend who was also a customer at a restaurant where I worked as a server in South Florida. This friend told me to write to John after I showed her my book, From the Projects to Princeton, which I carried in my apron while I tended tables. She was surprised to see what I'd done as I explained to her my story of incarceration and several setbacks. John and I met, chatted and he invited me to join his e-mail family. John Di Lemme has been a constant friend, a quiet mentor and steadfast encouragement for me. To this day, I hold him and his approach to success in high esteem."

- John I. Cook, Director
www.EducationalExcellence.net

"John is one of those bright lights, those naturals at what they do, that inspire you just to look at them, like watching a bird fly or a champion play any sport. My company has had the honor of having John on stage in front of our valued customers and business friends many times, and he always rocks their world bigger and better than anyone anticipated. He is the real deal. It's a privilege to learn what John has to teach about the power of Finding Your Why. He is a living example."

- Bruce Towers, President
www.FreedomBuildersInc.com

"John is a very unique motivator that is extremely passionate about assisting others to find their purpose in life. After listening to John, one can't help but get "Fired Up" about the concept of finding one's why and then soaring beyond one's perceived limits."

- Ellie Drake, Inspirational Speaker
www.BraveHeartProductions.com

"John Di Lemme knows what it takes to achieve personal greatness. In addition to being a living example himself, he's helped countless people both design and achieve success in their endeavors. Do yourself a favor and learn from him every chance you get!"

- Josh Hinds
www.GetMotivation.com

"John helped me understand that my products were better & worth more than my competition. I just needed to believe in myself, use his marketing strategies and implement them into my business. We made up a $3,000 program on Thursday & I sold one Friday. It was unreal! John helped me with a different kind of thinking pattern not just out of the box but out of the universe!"

- Cory Gregory, Fitness Trainer and Model
www.T3PersonalTraining.com

"My mentor and coach, John Di Lemme, has taught me to have FAITH in my Dream, take immediate focused action and never give up on my WHY".

- Frank Gasiorowski
www.90DayGoals.com

"I always knew I wanted a lot from my life. After achieving my professional career goals, the entrepreneurial spirit inside of me could not be suppressed. I was ready for the next chapter in my life, but I wasn't sure what. That's when I met John Di Lemme and grabbed a hold of John's "Find Your Why" CD. John taught me the importance of developing and writing down my Why and reading everyday. That roadmap combined with John's elite coaching has set me on a path of personal development and made it possible for me to build a successful, multi-million dollar business. Now, I am sharing my talents with others that want more from their lives and desire to become financially free."

- Violet Meuter, Entrepreneur

"John simply has a brilliance for developing people and finding what will energize their actions in Network Marketing. Anything that he has to say, I am writing down. It is solid gold!"

- Doug Firebaugh
www.PassionFire.com

Learn more about John's commitment to creating 1,000 Millionaires by visiting
www.FindYourWhy.com

Find Your Why and *Fly!*

The Ultimate Success Factor

JOHN DI LEMME

 **fulfillment Central**   Published by
FulfillmentCentral.com

Find Your Why ® and Fly! The Ultimate Success Factor
Copyright © 2005 by John Di Lemme

Di Lemme Development Group, Inc.
931 Village Boulevard
Suite 905 - 366
West Palm Beach, FL 33409-1939
877-277-3339
www.FindYourWhy.com

Book Design & Publishing:
Fulfillment Central Publishing, Inc.
808 Garmon Park Court
Loganville, GA 30052
info@fulfillmentcentral.com
www.FulfillmentCentral.com

ISBN 0-9769300-4-8

DEDICATION

My success is attributed to some very important people in my life. My parents, Philip and Mary Ann Di Lemme, raised me to be an honorable man and never take the easy way out. My grandfather, Philip Di Lemme, Sr., taught me the value of earning an honest income and that integrity is the foundation for a successful business. My brother, Mark Di Lemme, passed away at an early age and never had the chance to find his Why. My thoughts of him keep me focused on changing the lives of others and refusing to fail. My wife, Christie Di Lemme, is my rock and her unrelenting support reminds me daily that I am not alone in my quest to change the world. Her mother, Debbie Johnson, gave me her most precious gift, her daughter, and I am forever thankful. My business partner and best friend, Ed Zimbardi along with his wife, Brenda, and their entire family are the backbone of the DDG Team. Without these people in my life, I would not be here today, and it is my honor to dedicate this book to all of them.

-John Paul Di Lemme

CONTENTS

Foreword by Fritz Musser   xvii

Introduction   xix

Find Your Why and Fly - The Ultimate Success Factor Assessment
Visit - www.FindYourWhy.com/assessment ($797 Value)

FOREWORD

FRITZ MUSSER

Often I ask someone the question, "What could you do if you knew you could not fail?" Greatness lies within all people. The key is unlocking and releasing that greatness from within.

I have known John Di Lemme for many years and have personally witnessed his passion and drive for life and success. He is relentless in pursuing his "Why". You can believe that what he says will come to pass, because he never says it unless he believes it and he never gives up once he's says it. It's the power of your own words, and you can speak life or death with your words. John's words of life always come to fruition.

This book is a must for all to read. It doesn't matter where you are on the success ladder. You can be at the lowest point of your life or the highest point. Everybody has room for growth and improvement.

"Find Your Why and Fly" leads you strategically through the process of discovering your "Why" and cementing it into the fabric of your daily routine to personally experience what you once thought was difficult or impossible. John sees everyone as potential champions. He even says, "Champions make decisions and decisions make champions". You are a champion, and you have been given a "certificate for life" to become the best that you can be.

Now is the time for you to consume the powerful principles of this book, start your "Why Card" and get ready for the greatest season of your life. Your best days are ahead of you, and this book will place the tools in your life to accomplish greatness.

Learn more about John's commitment to creating 1,000 Millionaires by visiting
www.FindYourWhy.com

Catch the spirit of this book and what John Di Lemme has masterfully laid out for you. Read every page thoroughly. Do what he says and follow his advice. It will change your life forever. It is time for you to fly to greater levels of success and life. Enjoy the journey!

-Fritz Musser
www.TheTabernacle.org

INTRODUCTION

At the age of eighteen, I was diagnosed as a stutterer and labeled by society as handicapped. Little did I know that my stuttering would turn out to be a precious gift in my life. This so-called handicap became the driving force behind me creating the #1 most powerful success key in life...the development of a personal "Why."

Your "Why" is the reason that you do what you do everyday. From the moment you wake up, your personal guidance system that embodies your "Why" takes over. Your "Why" creates your attitude for the day that allows you to face life's challenges, overcome obstacles and successfully complete all of the goals that you have set for that day and beyond.

Your "Why" is your purpose for living. It identifies (and then guides you toward) your ultimate goal in life.

At the tender age of eighteen, I had no clue about my "Why" in life or what I wanted to do with the rest of my life. At the time, I was working around the clock at my family's art gallery. I worked there, because it was low-risk, easy, and convenient.

Over time, I became tired of just going through life and not actually living it. So, like many of you, I became a "looker". I was like a man in jail looking for a chance to escape. I was looking to make a run for real change and became desperate to release the success maniac inside of me.

Most successful people that I've met

★

I was looking to make a run for real change and became desperate to release the success maniac inside of me.

★

became desperate "lookers" at some critical point in their lives. Their desire to want something more out of life leads to their success. Are you a looker? If so, you may have the same problem I encountered in my looking. I truly knew what I wanted, but I didn't have the vehicle (the means of transportation) to accomplish it. **Over the last several years, I have seen so many people set goals and work very hard but never achieve them. Are you one of those people? The reason that you don't achieve your goals is because you are missing the vehicle, which is the driving force that will ultimately transport you to your desired results.**

I am blessed to deliver my messages to audiences around the globe and meet thousands of wonderful people but I've noticed something that deeply disturbs me every time that I speak. Many of the event attendees continually go from seminars to conferences to conventions investing thousands of dollars in personal development materials yet NEVER achieve the results that they desire in their lives. It breaks my heart to see good people striving to reach their goals and dreams but end up failing time and time again. Why does this happen? These champions simply don't have the vehicle to get them to where they want to go in life.

Now, I ask you to be totally honest with yourself. Have you ever been in a situation where you seemed to have a life-changing breakthrough, but you eventually just fell back in the same, unchanged, unproductive habits? Didn't it frustrate you to invest your precious time and your hard-earned money without getting the results that you desired? I've got good news for you! It can be so easy to achieve what you desire deep in your heart, and you can do it without wasting anymore of your time and your money. This is the vehicle that I've been referring to that will catapult you to success.

Live *Monday Night Motivational* Tele Class 8:30 p.m. EST.
Dial: 212-990-8000 - Access Code: 7458# - ($497 Value)

The secret that I will share in this book is not known by the general public. They don't know it, because we live in a fast paced, microwave society that suffers information overload. We want everything quick and easy in which we end up skimming over new information – even information that can save our life! It's like a rock skipping across a pond that eventually sinks without ever reaching its destination.

What I have to share with you has made thousands worldwide wake up and rethink their lives. Decide today to make an appointment with yourself and this book. Don't laugh. We all need to treat ourselves with as much respect as we treat others with whom we make appointments. This is your life that we're talking about! Have enough respect for yourself and your future to schedule quality time – with no cell phones, email or other distractions – in order to carve out a brand new life and path to success.

This powerful magic force that you are about to unlock will only work for you when you give it some time to release all its explosive power. Time is the most valuable currency we have. That's right. Nothing else in all of life has the value of time. You must be willing to invest time in your quest from where you are now to a life full of abundance. Do you truly want to live your dreams and achieve your goals? This is a question that only you can answer. If your answer is "yes", then read this book.

> ★
> *This powerful magic force that you are about to unlock will only work for you when you give it some time to release all its explosive power.*
> ★

Learn more about John's commitment to creating 1,000 Millionaires by visiting www.FindYourWhy.com

But, only when you have made an appointment with yourself and your destiny!

CHAPTER ONE

THE MOST IMPORTANT DAY OF YOUR LIFE

As life goes on day by day, we all experience challenging days and some really magnificent days, but there's one day in particular that is more important than any other day of your life. The most important day of your life is your birthday.

Why? At birth, we all start out the same. We are all on equal playing ground. Yes, I know we're all born into different external circumstances, but your birth certificate gives you the right to grow up and become a Champion. Your birth certificate is your "Certificate of Life". Unlike a college degree, you automatically earn your Certificate of Life when you exit the womb. No questions asked . . . you are destined for success.

Sounds easy, but that's where most people fall through the cracks. Even equipped with this wonderful certificate that gives them the right to achieve miracles and become a Champion, many fail to do so. Why? They simply don't take the action that makes their success possible. Let me give you an example. It's like someone that has been given a million dollar trust at birth, but they never write the check to unlock the funds. Now, does that make sense? No, but neither does having a "Certificate of Life" that enables you to create miracles and then you simply choose not to use it. You and only you are ultimately responsible for your level of success or failure in life.

Your mind and your heart are like a parachute. There's only one way that they work – they must be open! An open mind and an open heart will allow the dream inside of you that develops throughout your life to become a reality. Your birth certificate (aka your Certificate of Life) gives you the right to achieve your dreams. From the moment of your birth, you are destined for massive success, monumental prosperity and an incredible amount of unbelievable results in your life. But, you control the chances of when or how or if that will happen.

Once again, every single person has the same starting point in life. It's guaranteed. It's not a 60-day, 90-day, 120-day or even a 60,000 mile guarantee. It is a lifetime guarantee! You are guaranteed at birth that you have the same ability to achieve success as everyone else. Your race, your gender and/or your physical handicaps don't matter. It's simply your decision of whether or not you achieve this success. Remember, Champions Make Decisions and Decisions Make Champions.

★

You are guaranteed at birth that you have the same ability to achieve success as everyone else.

★

You are Not a Victim

Let me explain what I mean here. We live in an age of "victimization". We've been trained to think and live as victims. Our whole culture is saturated with messages that "you cannot achieve because . . ." Some see themselves as victims of ethnicity, gender, being born into a low-income family, vast conspiracies, etc. If you regularly watch the evening news or brainwash yourself with other forms of negative, popular culture, then that victim mentality will become ingrained in your mind. That's why I advise people to avoid those messages and watch movies like "Cinderella Man" that reinforce the positive aspects of life and make you believe that you can achieve success despite the challenges that you face.

Victimization is a lie! Notice how victimization always relates to people as "groups", but you and I are individuals. *We are not groups!* That's how the lie gets instilled. When you see yourself as part of a group (racial, economic, social, religious, etc.), then you begin to see your destiny as something that is out of your own hands. You jump on the bandwagon of failure, because you think that your future is already written according to the lives of others. That kind of deception keeps people from taking responsibility for and ownership of their own destiny.

Just Do It!

You are an individual created by God and given a wide-open path to success. Take your birth certificate as a Certificate of Life that gives you as an individual the permission and the right to be successful.

Now, stand up and say out loud, ***"I am a certified champion by birthright. My certificate of life gives me the right to achieve success."*** Say it again, but this time say it with true conviction. Say it with power and with genuine belief that you know it is true! You must believe before you can achieve. Go ahead, say it over and over and over until you do believe that you can achieve massive results in your life.

When Jesus was in his earthly ministry, he often told people to do outrageous things. For example, he told his disciples to catch a fish and cut it open in order to find the money to pay taxes. Another time, he told them to go borrow a donkey. He also instructed a blind man to go wash in a particular pool of water to regain his sight. Would you say those are outrageous actions? Why did he do those things? Because he knew that when people actually do outrageous things, they unlock a dimension of power with themselves that they didn't even know existed.

This kind of power created by taking action blows the doors off the prison of passivity. Taking bold action is explosive power! It will often take us from a "do nothing" realm onto the higher ground of action, engagement and success. That's the reason that I often ask people to take specific action steps. As long as we just merely think, feel or believe, we remain passive. There's no action in thinking, feeling and believing. Have you ever been in a situation when you really want to do something that you know will change your life, but you think "Oh, that would be silly to do that. I'm not going to embarrass myself. What would people think of me?" As long as you let those types of feelings and beliefs control your ability to act on something, you will remain in a prison of doubt and fear.

I like the old Nike advertising line: "Just do it."

Trust me: there is a great and priceless value associated with just doing it.

But when you take action and do something that you know will make a difference in your life, a new realm of power begins to work inside. Throughout the journey of this book, I will ask you to take action steps like standing up, speaking words out loud and writing down specific exercises. I like the old Nike advertising line: "Just do it". Trust me. There is a great and priceless value associated with just doing it without over thinking it.

WARNING: I will challenge you to get out of your comfort zone, and this will make you uncomfortable at times. But no matter what, you must commit to completing all exercises and get beyond passivity and embarrassment. Once you learn to do this, nothing will be able to stop you from taking the action needed to achieve your dreams in life.

Once more, I want you to say out loud, "I am committed to my success". Do you believe that? Say it over and over and over until you DO believe it. If you cannot do that, then you will not succeed. Don't go any further in your reading until you have made this commitment to yourself!

Time to Use Your "Certificate of Life"

Now, I'm going to ask you to do something else. Go get a copy of your birth certificate, laminate it and put it on your desk (or the dashboard of your car, the cockpit of your plane or any other work site). I call your work area "the construction zone". Why? Because we are going to BUILD your future!

We will even develop blueprints along the journey that will lead to your future success. It's like building a skyscraper. There is a starting point for the visionary architect. He must know the purpose, style, height and other dimensions of the building and what supplies will be needed in the construction. Well guess what? Your birth certificate is your starting point. So, let's take action and begin building your future. You will look at your birth certificate everyday and remember that you are an individual not a group and that you have the right to be successful in every area of your life.

Decision plus action equals results. We need to recreate the daily process that creates your results. Every day is a phenomenal day. That's why it's called the "present". *You must treat everyday like a "present", and open it with great expectation. Live each day as if it's a precious gift, because it is!* Don't proceed any further with your reading until you have your Certificate of Life in front of you so that you see it every day. It serves as a reminder that you can and will achieve monumental success.

Reprogram Your Life

Now that you have your "Certificate of Life" in front of you, I want you to look at it and say, "It's all my fault". That's right. *Your life is your fault – good or bad.* I can almost hear the chorus of readers now: "What do you mean, John? Why would you tell me that it's all my fault?" Okay, okay, it's actually your default.

Let me explain. As many of you know, I have a New York accent. I have a New York accent, because I grew up around New Yorkers. From the date of your birth until approximately the age of seven, your default in life is developed. Yes, it's a little confusing at first so let me explain further.

When you purchase a computer, it comes with certain programs that give it the ability to function when you turn it on. After you "boot up", you choose new software, your internet provider and other technical features in order to make it suitable for you. But unless you successfully install and "save" your new software, your computer will always revert back to those original default settings. That is, unless you make a decision to change those defaults by saving your new programs.

By the age of seven, your mental computer had all its defaults developed and installed on your hard drive. Think about that. How many times were you told as a young child, "Stop. Don't do that. Don't touch that. Don't talk to strangers. Stay away from them. Don't look at that. Don't, don't, don't, don't?"

You are told "don't" and "do not" and "stop" about 17 million times versus the word "yes". This default is not only "installed" by your parents as a young child, but also your grandparents, relatives, babysitters, teachers, friends and anyone else that you may have spent time with growing up.

Your default setting creates doubt instead of hope for a successful future. So, when it comes to a decisive stage in your life and you step out in faith, you must understand that you are challenging your default.

Your default setting creates doubt instead of hope for a successful future. So when it comes to a decisive stage in your life and you step out in faith, you must understand that you are challenging your default.

How do you change this? Just like you change a computer to make it more suitable to your own purposes and dreams, you have to "install and save" your own software in which you change your default settings and reboot.

How do you do this? Eastern cultures understand the power of the spoken word much more than Americans do. When we speak words, those words take on a life of their own. Just as negative words spoken by others when we were younger have deep power in our lives so do positive words. A major part of "installing" our own software is found in the beautiful and magical mystery of speaking positive, life-affirming, "future-positive" words.

Simply speak affirmations that empower you to believe in yourself and the achievement of your goals, dreams and desires. You have the right to success, and you will succeed in the game of life! You must switch your default from "no, no, no" to "yes, yes, yes". This is not easy, because you are unlearning behaviors that have been on your hard drive since the day you were born.

If you are forty years old, then that's four decades of negative defaults that you must reprogram. Not easy to do. It doesn't happen overnight, and it usually doesn't happen by reading one book. You must invest in personal success habits on a daily basis that break through those defaults that were cemented in your childhood.

I along with most educators believe that you must read or listen to something at least seven times before you truly grasp the concepts of the material. Why? Because we are a society of multi-taskers. This means that we often do several things at one time; therefore, we don't pay enough attention to any one thing and often miss the importance of what we are reading or listening to.

I suggest that you invest in seven different colored highlighters prior to reading this book. The first time that you read it, grab one highlighter and highlight what jumps out at you. Then, use a different color each time that you read it. I think you will be surprised at how much you missed the last time. You will also see that you internalize the reading differently on the 2nd, 3rd, 4th and successive readings because of the growth in your life.

Before our journey continues, we are going to begin recreating your defaults. Remember, this is a constant battle, and many people give up. Your default settings are very strong so you need to be very strong in re-programming your life. Let's get started!

I want you to commit right now to doing this exercise every time you are led to fall back into your negative defaults. You must say out loud, *"I am a Champion by birthright, and I will not let my negative defaults control my successful future."* Will you do this? Make a commitment right now to yourself by writing that affirmation out below:

Your default settings are very strong. So, you need to be very strong in re-programming your life. Let's get started!

I AM a Champion !
By Birthright & I will
not let my negative defaults
control my successful future!
8/8/2010
Wellington, FL

Say it one more time just to get you comfortable with resetting your defaults. *"I am a Champion by birthright and I will not let my negative defaults control my successful future!"*

Kick the Chicken

Your negative defaults also known as "the past" will control your future only if YOU let them. The past tends to bind shackles around your ankles that hold you down as you try to proceed on your success journey. Close your eyes and imagine five hundred pound chains around each of your ankles as your pursuing your dream. It's impossible! You and only you can make the decision to rip the chains of your past (your default

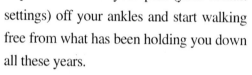

settings) off your ankles and start walking free from what has been holding you down all these years.

You and only you can make the decision to rip the chains of your past (your default settings) off your ankles and start walking free from what has been holding you down all these years.

Many years ago, a minister gave a great illustration of this truth. He said that when farmers take chickens to the market, they will often tie their ankles and lay them in the bed of their truck for the ride to the sale barn. This prevents them from flying out of the truck.

When they arrive at the sale barn, he will take them out of the truck, place them on the ground, and then cut the cords, releasing them to get up. But, chickens won't get up! They think they're still bound at their ankles, so they just lay there. The farmer has to actually kick them to stir them to flutter and get up. He went on to say that we must "kick the chicken" in ourselves in order to get out of our incapacities. So, "kick the chicken" in yourself. Your ankles are free!

As you go forward, don't use your past to determine your future. Do not make excuses based on your past. Burn the bridge to your past mistakes and limitations. ***Remember:*** *If the bridge to your past is burned behind you, then you have no choice but to travel the path into a successful future*. Develop your Why in life and begin to achieve things in life that you only dreamed about. Choosing success over failure is your decision.

Champion Affirmations

"I am a winner and a champion! I am beautiful. I am a goal achiever, and I am going to be rich! Today will affect my future."

- Lucy G., United Kingdom (16 years old)

"I am a Champion! I can do this. I am a master with money. I am a Multi-Millionaire, Miracle-Making Woman!"

– Beverley J., Canada

"I am a fear demolishing, obstacle crushing, profit producing, warrior of God that is destined for success enabling others to achieve their hopes, dreams and desires."

- Barrie G., United Kingdom

"Go get it! The sky is not the limit."

– Lina R., Fiji Islands

"I am a champion, and I am fired up!"

– Leanne W., Australia

Are you a member of the world famous Motivational Club?
www.FindYourWhy.com/club

"I am a person of value, and I take action. I make wise decision. I demolish all fears. I am pursuing my purpose with commitment, passion and perseverance. I am a goal achiever. I know my Why. I am walking in divine health. I am walking in divine favor. I am building a world wide team of financially free leaders that are impacting their families, nations and countries, financially, spiritually and socially. I am fearfully and wonderfully made. I am implementing the habits that will take me to my destiny. I am a Multi-Millionaire Champion!"

– *Jacqueline C., Bahamas*

"I am a victorious, world shaker, action taker, fear demolishing, champion! I am a winner! Fired up!"

– *Vincentina O., Sweden*

"I am a champion! 2006 is best year ever. I have an attitude of gratitude."

– *Carol W., Georgia*

"I am the exception to the rule and a deviation from the norm. I am complete and whole to the fullest."

– *Calandra, J., Georgia*

"I am a champion. I am born for greatness. I am living my dreams. I am going to the next level. I am demolishing fear. I am building faith. I am producing income. I am giving back. I am making a difference. I am stepping up, stepping out and stepping on fear. I am living to my utmost potential. I am reclaiming my destiny that I was born to receive."

- Luci P., Georgia

"I am going for it! I am strong and no matter what I am going to build my dream!"

– Maria M., Malta

"I can do this business! Other people succeed; so can I. I deserve a fantastic lifestyle."

– Liz M., United Kingdom

"I am a champion recruiter! I am successful. I am prosperous. I am fired up. I am born for greatness. I am living my dreams. I am going to the next level. I am demolishing fear. I am building faith. I am producing income. I am giving back. I am making a difference. I am stepping up, stepping out and stepping on fear. I am living to my utmost potential. I am reclaiming my destiny that I was born to receive!"

– Jean F., Minnesota

Live *Monday Night Motivational* Tele Class 8:30 p.m. EST.
Dial: 212-990-8000 - Access Code: 7458# - ($497 Value)

"I am a good mother that devotes quality time to her kids. My family is the most important thing in my life. I read books and scriptures to my children. I am loving and patient. I expect a miracle each day and miracles are really happening in my life. I am changing lives. I am a champion. I am achieving my goals. I am going to build a solid residual income. I am going to make things happen. I am responsible for my own future. I deserve a better lifestyle. I am going to have a new van. I am going to take vacations with my family."

– *Dafne K., Mexico*

"I seek first the Kingdom of God and his righteousness. My life is an example of my Christian faith and of Jesus' ideals of love, witness, compassion, honesty, integrity and servant hood. I treat others as I would wish to be treated myself. I pursue my purpose with passion so I am growing along with my purpose. I am doing more and achieving more today, than I have ever done before for both myself and others. I choose to sow bountifully; therefore, I will reap bountifully. I am blessed and highly favored and have been called to be a blessing to others. No weapon formed against me or my business prospers. The Lord is a wall of fire around us, and he is the center of my life. Today with God, I am making a difference."

- *Michael P., United Kingdom*

"I am young at heart and an inspiration to others to live their lives to the fullest. I am happy. I am beautiful. I am healthy."

– *Christine S., United Kingdom*

"I am a warrior of God. I am a winner and leader. I am an eradicator of negativity, a winner of spiritual battles and a believer in achievement. I am living my dreams and creating more. I am defeating the enemy and in the top 3% life's achievers."

– *Sabina D., United Kingdom*

"I am a champion. I am a millionaire. I am getting better and better in prospecting, recruiting and duplicating my strengths. I am enjoying quality time with my daughter, living in a lovely apartment, driving a lovely car and going around the world learning about other cultures. I am enjoying great health and financial freedom, attracting great leaders in my country and around the world. I am building 5-10 millionaires in the next 5 to 10 years. I have a strong team. I am developing spiritually. I afford to give more than I receive."

- *Josette C., Malta*

"I am a child of God, and I am beautiful."

– *Connie & Rich A., Florida*

"Things are rocking. I am building my business. My life is changing. My finances are flowing abundantly. I am prosperous. I am living my dreams."

– Jan A., Canada

"I am a champion recruiter. I have a millionaire mindset. I am the leader that people are looking for. I can do all things through Christ who strengthens me. I am playing the game to win."

– Allison V., Utah

"Bye Bye fear...hello faith. I am a Champion. I am going to the next level. I am shocking my bank teller. I am one of John Di Lemme's millionaires. I am driving the car of my dreams. I am funding medical clinics for the poor. I am helping 100 people reach financial freedom. I am successful. I am prosperous. I am living my dreams. I am FIRED UP!"

– Maryann K., Connecticut

"I am a millionaire dream achiever! I am a success champion! I am attacking fear head on! I am exploding into success like a rocket! I am sharing with excitement! I am living my dreams! I am a decision maker! I expect and receive miracles! I am changing people's lives! I am a multi-millionaire! I am stepping out in faith! I am fired up and 110% focused!

Find Your Why and Fly - The Ultimate Success Factor Assessment
Visit - www.FindYourWhy.com/assessment ($797 Value)

I am the leader of my dreams! I am a dream connector!"

– *Diane T., Canada*

"I have a purpose to create the best in others and in myself, to inspire, to aspire and not to expire."

– *Kagwiria M., Kenya*

"Today will be a new day, different from the previous day. I adore Nature. I remember my good dreams. I thank God for whatever he has showered on me. ."

– *Hemlata C., India*

"I am Successful. I am Prosperous. I am living my dreams. I am Fired Up. My heart is smiling. My eyes are looking from sky. I can fly. I can walk. I must fly. I am Prosperous. I am living my dreams. I can give my fire as a present to other people. I am happy, because I am successful. I believe in myself. I am a Champion!"

– *Margarita N., Lithuania*

CHAPTER TWO

THE POWER OF COMMITMENT

Few things in life have as much power as commitment. Commitment turns average or inactive people into what the military calls a "full metal jacket" (a bullet that can penetrate great obstacles). The character trait of commitment does that. It gives our dreams the "full metal jacket" they need in order to punch through obstacles. In fact, I would say that *commitment is the foundation for building your life*. It is the bedrock of achieving your ultimate "Why" in life.

Let me ask you a question. Are you truly committed to the achieving your dreams and goals in life? I'm sure you said "Yes". Okay, let me ask you an easier question. Have you invested in the seven highlighters that I discussed in the last chapter?

If you haven't made the commitment to complete the exercises in chapter one of this book, then stop right now, go back and do it. You cannot expect to achieve the maximum results of this material if you are not committed to achieving these results. In order to achieve your ultimate goals and dreams in life, you must have a starting point and take action.

I know this sounds a little harsh, but as your coach I must and will hold you accountable for your actions and your failure to take action. My ultimate goal is to assist you in achieving your Why in life. At times, I am like a drill instructor whose purpose is to turn green recruits into full metal jackets. I am very serious about helping you to "Find Your Why and Fly". I hope you are serious enough to "just do it."

What is Commitment?

Commitment is a serious, even sacred, pledge to do or be something. It is hammer-hard determination to achieve. Like a full-metal jacket bullet, it is so focused on the goal that it blows right through the obstacles and distractions. Commitment takes us beyond comfort zones and personal indulgences. The Oxford English Dictionary defines commitment as "an engagement or obligation that restricts freedom of action."

Think about that. Being committed to a goal means we have to give up some of our freedom. For example, if I'm committed to investing 20% of my income, then I may have to give up the freedom to buy all the latest electronic toys. If I'm going to lose forty pounds in the next six months, then I may be forced to give up my freedom to have a glass of milk and cookies before I go to bed.

Are you committed – REALLY COMMITTED – to your own success? Is that commitment strong enough to finish reading this book? Be honest. How many books have you bought and not read? How many books have you cracked open, read a few pages or chapters and then stuck on the shelf?

Now, I'm going to challenge you to read every chapter and every word of this book. Upon completion of reading each chapter of this book, write a summary of it in your learning journal. A learning journal doesn't have to be anything fancy. A basic notebook will do. It is critically important to write down what really hits you out of each chapter. I also refer to this as "brain-spilling". Regularly and frequently summarizing each chapter is the best way to get life-changing truth off the page and into your heart and mind. By reading it, writing it down and reviewing it frequently, you internalize it. You take possession of it. You take ownership of the truth that will set you free!

Remember, I said earlier that we must all read or listen to something at least seven times before we truly grasp the concepts of the material. You should also write in your journal each time you re-read it. You will see that each time you read the book, your journal will reflect different thoughts and ideas that will dramatically change your life if you commit to them. Even the seventh time!

What will Commitment Do in My Life?

I believe that commitment is the key to achieving the level of success that your certificate of life guarantees. Not only is commitment a full metal jacket, it is also life's cement.

Strong foundations are not made of sand. A foundation must be strong enough to hold everything stable and steady during a storm or earthquake. That's why foundations are made of cement. Your commitment to achieve your dreams is your life's cement.

Your commitment, your pledge, to achieve your dreams is your life's cement. When you have a cement commitment behind your dreams, nothing will stop you.

When you have a cement commitment behind your dreams, nothing will stop you. You will stand tall through the storms of life and create a safe atmosphere for yourself and your family. When everyone else says it's impossible and you will fail, your personal commitment provides another voice. That voice says, *"You will persevere and win!"*

How to Maintain Your Commitment

Over time, even cement will crack and break. Think about strolling down a sidewalk and looking down to see the weeds growing between the cracks. Your life's foundation can also crack and allow weeds to grow. These "weeds" are often the naysayers and the critics that don't believe in you or your right to achieve success.

Repairs are essential to keeping your commitment foundation strong. *If you don't create and maintain a strong cement foundation of commitment in your life, then you will allow the negative weeds to get between you and your dreams.*

How do you maintain your commitment? *First,* you must read and re-read the right books and write in your journal each time that you read them. Books like Napoleon Hill's "Think and Grow Rich" or George S. Clason's "The Richest Man in Babylon" or the one that you're holding are great assets to your success library.

Second, spend time with successful, positive, encouraging people. Some people just radiate success, confidence and commitment. Hanging out with them will help to maintain your own foundation of commitment. When you spend time with negative, doubtful, mistrusting people, you will damage your foundation.

Jim Rohn, one of my mentors, says that we should regularly ask ourselves, "Who am I with? What are they doing to me? Is that good?" I agree. You've got to commit to yourself that you will not hang out with and be a victim of "dream stealers".

No one but YOU owns the title deed to your life. Out of respect for yourself, commit to spending time with those who are victors in life. *Be committed to walking in victory!*

Third, forget the mistakes and negative defaults of the past. You're free! "Kick your chicken" leaving your shackles of the past behind.

You must be determined to develop your commitment long term, because success is not easy. Failure is guaranteed if you are not committed to your success. Daily commitment to the achievement of your Why will push you through the trials of life. It's like physical exercise; it must be done daily.

An essential part of maintaining your commitment is to stay away from cynics and dream stealers. Join with others in walking in victory! Don't let negative people determine your level of success.

If you read the right books, journal your thoughts, spend time with positive, successful people and leave your past mistakes behind, you will find that your

> *No one but YOU owns the title deed to your life. Out of respect for yourself, commit to spending time with those who are victors in life. Join with others in walking in victory! Don't let negative people determine your level of success.*

foundation of commitment will harden just like cement and become stronger each day.

Think about it for a second. When cement is first poured, it is not hard. Sometimes people will put their name in it or mark it in some way while it is wet. Once the cement is hardened, it remains that way forever with proper maintenance. In the same way, once your commitment hardens in your mind and heart, it will remain that way. It's up to you to keep the naysayers, your negative past and other discouraging factors from defacing your commitment before it is hardened into a strong foundation in your heart and mind.

I'm a New Yorker, but I like the song of the wide-open West, "Home on the Range". I like it mainly because of one line, "where never is heard a discouraging word". Think about that. Do you care enough about your own success to live in an environment that contains no discouragement? Are you so committed to your future that you will surround yourself with people, books and movies that encourage, rather than discourage you?

Never forget that the power of your commitment is one of the greatest factors in your life. Your commitment to success or your commitment to your cycle of failure will determine whether or not you achieve your life long dream. Let's try to understand this. The word power means the authority to take control over. *You need to take control and authority over your lack of commitment in the past and recommit to your achievement of your goals and dreams.*

If you are a success maniac, then commit yourself to your own future. This type of commitment gives you both the right and the power to achieve your ultimate Why in life. Behind every Champion's achievement of their Why is a strong and solid commitment. When you're on track and have commitment as hard as cement, your foundation doesn't move around. Yes, you're "hard-headed". You're solid as a rock! You are going for it! You're making decisions like a committed Champion!

That's where it all starts to come together and before you know it, your life takes off like a space shuttle and people standing around suddenly jump back, look startled and say, "Whoa! What happened? What's going on with you?" What they're seeing is the blast-off of your success rocket, the manifestation of your commitment.

That's why commitment is one of the most important keys to success. Remember, your commitment is the foundation, and it's your decisions that will determine whether or not your foundation will crack in the midst of life's storms.

Now, I want you to write out your commitment. Write down what you are committed to doing with the rest of your life and what obstacles you are committed to avoiding.

Champion Commitments

"I am completely committed to immersing myself in personal development so that I can share what I've learned with others, particularly my children (age 8 & 9). I want to give them the knowledge to do anything they want and not have stressful, health depleting jobs. I am determined to overcome obstacles like negative people, my own past and personal struggles that get in the way of my success."

– *Marina A., United Kingdom*

"I am committed to getting street kids off the street through my gifts in training, coaching and music. Money will no longer be an obstacle that prevents me from helping these children."

– *Jacob P., United States*

"I am a health enhancing warrior that is committed to assisting others with taking control of their minds and bodies by building their dreams and enhancing their spirits. I will not let the negativity of others break this commitment."

– *Steve H., United Kingdom*

"I am committed to becoming a hugely, successful business woman and will build a multi-million dollar business. My biggest obstacle is rejection by naysayers, and I refuse to let those people steal my dream."

– *Jasmine S., United Kingdom*

"My commitment is based on attracting ambitious, self-motivated and active builders into my business. I will not give others permission to squash my dreams of building a multi-million dollar dynasty."

– *Naheed B., United Kingdom*

"I am committed to raising the bar and bringing more value to my-self so that I can bring more value to others. I will continue to show the plan and create wealth builders. I will no longer be hindered by obstacles and will take massive, consistent action to prevent these roadblocks from stopping me from achieving my Why."

– *Allison V., Utah*

"I am committed to facing my fears and overcoming adversity."

– *Zep P., Missouri*

"I am committed to being a champion in all that I do, and do all that I can do to be a champion. I am committed to My Why, doing daily personal coaching, self-improvement, reading, and listening to CDs/ DVDs, doing physical exercises, updating my dream wall, talking positive all of the time and breathing my dream. The obstacles I am committed to overcome are self-sabotaged, negative people putting me down, the thought that I am not worthy of wealth, financial freedom and happiness."

– Kenneth T., Malta

"I am committed to a life of service. Obstacles are everywhere; however, I love a challenge and enjoy plowing through them. If fear arises, then I will take on what I'm afraid of. If people try to discourage me, then I will continue to love them and move forward."

– Annette R., Utah

"My commitment is to my family and myself. I face each day with the goal of being an exceptional wife and mother. I am blessed with a wonderful family, and I delight in their existence each and every day. I take pride in myself and know that I will fulfill my Why in life."

– Mary S., New York

CHAPTER THREE

THE HABIT OF GIVING

People often ask me things like, "John, what is the main habit of multi-million dollar entrepreneurs, life-changers and dream achievers?" There is no question at all in my mind that the number one habit of all of those people is giving.

Before we move on to discuss the ultimate success factor, which is the manifestation and development of your Why in life, I want to discuss this one habit that will have a great impact on your level of success. It's the habit of giving.

As you begin developing your Why and reading other Champion Why Cards in this book, you will see that many people like you want to help others by giving away a percentage of their success. When I read some of my student's Why Cards, I see things like "I want to donate $10,000.00 dollars to my favorite charity" or "I want to tithe $50,000.00 to my church".

I believe that we are all born with the desire to bless others. We all want to give back. We have an inbred need to make other people's lives better. I believe that we are created in God's image, and he is very generous. Therefore, it's only reasonable to believe that we as human beings are generous. It's only the negative scripts in our society like "always look out for number one" that turn us from generous to selfish.

I've learned that the best exercise in the world is to reach down and lift someone up. The sad thing is that we lose sight of helping others when we are so focused on ourselves. You really do want to give financial blessings to others. You want to give your time, and you long to invest your energy in noble causes. Based on your need as a human being to give to others, you must make the decision to include the habit of giving time, money and energy in your Why.

The Mystery of Sowing and Reaping

───── ★ ─────

We cannot sow a selfish attitude and expect to reap abundance and generosity. It just doesn't work like that. If we make giving a habit, then life has a way of giving back to us. All successful people know and practice that exact concept.

───── ★ ─────

I know that you may not be accustomed to giving freely, especially when you have never had that much to give. It's uncomfortable at first, but the giving habit makes you a stronger person. I truly believe that you will sow what you reap. Most people are familiar with that principle or at least that phrase, but think about what it means.

If you sow wheat in a field, the crop that pushes through the soil to be harvested is wheat. It is not and will never be corn. If you plant an apple seed, the green shoot that springs from the ground will not become a pecan tree.

We cannot sow a selfish attitude and expect to reap abundance and generosity.

It just doesn't work like that. Once again, if we make giving a habit, then life has a way of giving back to us. All successful people even non-religious ones know and practice that exact concept. If we make giving a habit, then life has a way of giving back to us. That knowledge is one of the greatest commonalities of all successful people.

Trust me. If you make the habit of giving a main priority in your life, then you will be blessed beyond all of your goals and dreams that you have ever imagined of achieving.

Now, let's get you started on your habit of giving by saying the following out loud: "I am a daily giver. I will commit to giving daily to others". Repeat this statement over and over until you truly internalize it.

How to Get Started in the Habit of Giving

Obviously, you don't start out by distributing one hundred dollar bills as you walk down the street. You can give in many ways. Here are a few ways you can start to cultivate this new habit:

- Donate your time to your favorite organization or a friend in need.
- Offer your wisdom to person that may be starting a new life for himself/herself.
- Smile and say hello to someone that looks like they really need something positive to happen to them.
- Take some of your old clothes that you never wear to the Salvation Army or local shelter.
- Cook a hot meal for an elderly shut-in.
- Repair an automobile for someone that can't afford the repairs.

I would say that the first rule of giving is very simple...give what you have. If you don't have wealth, you may not be able to give money, but you can still be a giver. You can still cultivate the habit of giving.

First, give whatever you have been blessed with or whatever talent you have. You have to sow these seeds today in order to design your future. You design and predict your future by planting seeds in the lives of others. If you plant seeds of hope in others, then you will reap a bountiful harvest (a successful future).

Of course, there's a flip side to that. If you are selfish and only think of getting what you want out of life, then you will reap what you sow – selfishness. Your failure to plant seeds in the lives of others will result in nothing but dried up soil not to mention a very lonely and unfulfilled life.

There's nothing better than the feeling you have after you have blessed the life of another person. For instance, my wife and I decided three years ago not to give Christmas gifts to each other and even asked our family/friends not to give us Christmas gifts. Instead, we take the money that everyone would have spent on those gifts and provide a great Christmas for families in need. Christmas is our favorite time of the year not because of what we receive, but because of what we give away and the joy that our giving brings to others.

Anyone Can Give

Some of you will say, "You know what John? I just can't give right now because I have nothing to give." You're wrong. A smile is a gift. A handshake or an embrace is a seed. Being there with a shoulder to cry on is a seed. Being accountable to your business partner is a seed. Being a daily giver of seeds will change the face of your future.

Don't be misled. Remember that you can't ignore God and get away with it. You will always reap what you sow!".
- Galatians 6:7

Always remember, "Seasons come and seasons go, but seedtime and harvest will not cease no matter what we do." Think of it this way. If you plant a seed in the summer, then you will reap its fruits in the fall. If you fail to plant a seed in the summer, then in the fall you will have no harvest. The great Jim Rohn says, "Everyone must be good at sowing in the spring or will be begging in the fall".

The habit of giving is like insurance for the achievement of our ultimate "Why" in life. For example, if you have a car accident, then your insurance guarantees that your damages will be covered based on the amount that you provided in your policy. It's the same with giving. Your habit of giving determines your level of success in your future; it is based on what you have given away.

Many people think that they will wait until they are a multi-millionaire to give. That is not the way to start. The sad reality is that if you can't bring yourself to give now, then you sure won't make yourself give when you are financially secure and wealthy. Remember, giving is an attitude. It is not based on the amount of money in your bank account. It's a heart issue. That's why I say that anyone can give.

You Can Only Keep What You Give Away

I heard an incredible true story that I want to pass on to you. A strong couple had not been married very long when the husband began to feel a strong sense that they should give away their household possessions, which included furniture, appliances and even their wedding gifts. Everything! After a few days, he reluctantly shared his feelings with his young wife only to discover that she had a very strong sense of the same thing. She had been struggling with how to tell him.

Confident that God was directing them, they began the process of giving everything away. Within a few days, everything was gone. The husband recalls, "Even the original painting that my grandmother had painted, a family heirloom, was given away". Although somewhat perplexed as they slept on the floor amidst nothing, they felt peace and assurance that they had done the right thing.

If we hoard our treasures, then they shrivel and disappear. If we give them away, then they return to us.

A few weeks later as they were driving home, they saw smoke rising from the landscape. As they drove closer to their neighborhood, they realized the smoke was billowing up from their property. Their house was consumed by flames and burned to the ground.

A few nights later after they had settled into temporary housing, car lights appeared in their driveway. A friend walked to the front door carrying the gift that this young couple had presented to him a few weeks earlier. During the next few days, a steady stream of cars came to their home returning nearly every item they had given away.

Years later, the husband said a very profound thing, "We learned at any early age that you can only keep what you give away. Today, we once again treasure my grandmother's painting. It only hangs in our home because we once gave it away".

That is so true. If we hoard our treasures, then they shrivel and disappear. If we give them away, then they return to us. Learn to create the *daily* habit of giving, and at the conclusion of your day ask yourself, "What did I do today? What seed did I plant today in order to predict my future?" Remember, whatsoever you sow you shall reap.

I want to ask you a bold and provocative question: "If you sow nothing, then how can you have the audacity to expect something in return?" That would be like not planting any seeds in your field, but expecting a corn harvest. First comes the seeds that you plant, and then comes your harvest. Never forget that.

Plant something every day! Do not end your day without giving something away whether it's a smile, a big tip to a waitress, a dollar to a homeless man, a huge tithe to your church, etc. Give someone the op-portunity to have their life changed by you being a better person.

Understand this. You are a uniquely privileged individual simply, because you are holding this book in your hand. Millions have lived and died without ever finding the secrets to success. Be grateful for all that has flowed to you and from that gratitude bless others. Allow them to reap some of the rewards of you (*the Champion*) by developing the habit of giving.

If you read about the truly wealthy entrepreneurs like John D. Rockefeller and Mary Kay Ash, you will see that those Champions passed away giving away more than they earned, which means they started the process of giving early in their careers. When the famous Pastor W. A. Criswell of First Baptist Church of Dallas retired, he gave the church a check that was more than all the salary checks he had ever received. I challenge you to model your life after those great people by developing the habit of giving today.

Write down how you will begin the habit of giving. What will you give away on a daily basis? How will you impact the lives of others?

Champion Givers

"We (*my wife and I*) are almost giving 10% of our income to our church and charities. We are receptive to giving more our time and monies to missions and local needs of our community. Financial freedom would be an added privilege to assist to these needs."

– *Randy T., Illinois*

"I impact the lives of others through giving by being an example through my actions, devoting time to hear what they have to say and projecting motivation."

– *Michelle M., Malta*

"I impact other peoples live with my time by listening to them and in which I hear their views. Money has only provides limited satisfaction when giving to others. We have to start growing from the inside to become true millionaires on the outside to others."

– *Kagwiria M., Kenya*

"Today I impact lives of others more than I ever dreamed, because I am a teacher. Everyday I meet young people that need my knowledge, my advice and my coaching. They always want to believe that teacher knows all in the world. I share my time, my energy, my creations and my views on life with them. Why? Because they are young champions that will someday change the world."

– *Magarita N., Lithuania*

"We are currently sponsoring 3 children monthly – in Africa, Philippines and El Salvador and have for many years supported missionaries in 3rd World Countries. We donate to well drilling projects and our local church. Our children both tithe faithfully from their allowance, gift money and any money they earn for extra chores. Our young son also donates 50% of business profits from his 3 businesses to various children's projects. Our family is very busy but each one gives of their time somehow. My husband is an assistant Baseball Coach. I teach ice skating to adult Special Olympians, help out at several churches and contribute to a women's health and fitness forum. Our daughter is volunteering with a young skating team as well as belonging to her school's youth action organization and volunteering at many skating competitions and races. Our son is a volunteer monitor at school plus helps out at skating competitions and races."

– *Jan A., Canada*

"I impact the life of others by giving them love, support and strength. My gift of time is worth it when I manage to give others just a simple kiss of positivity that ultimately changes their entire day."

– Maria M., Malta

"I am a generous giver by spending time with others and treating them with the respect that they deserve."

– Vincentina O., Sweden

"I take what I learn from my mentors and cultivate others when they are in need of a sprinkle of motivational nourishment. People come to me just to be motivated and encouraged. I send out an inspirational/ motivational quote each day. I do the same with those that I mentor by encouraging them to open their minds to dream and vision greatness within themselves. It's a must for me to challenge the youth with greater possibilities and cheer them on when great things happen in their lives."

- Calandra J., Georgia

"It's easy to impact other people's lives. All that you have to do is believe in yourself and you will become a mirror that reflects acts of service, devotion and love."

– Dafne B., Mexico

I donate yearly to charities of my choice like Canuck Place that supports children with terminal disease. I do this in honor of my two brothers that loved hockey and children. I also run races that have charitable organizations attached that I respect and wish to support. I have worked in the medical diagnostic profession for about 30 years and continue to treat my patients with the respect and compassion that they deserve. I have volunteered at numerous races to give back to the running community that supported me through my many years of running races, marathons and a triathlon. I have volunteered in the medical tent at Ironman Penticton for six years to give back to the Ironman community that supported me and to say thank you to the medical staff at Ironman for my medical care when I hit a crisis point in one of my Ironman Events."

- Beverley J., Canada

CHAPTER FOUR

WHY IS IT ALL ABOUT THE "WHY"?

Yes, you read it right. Why is it all about the "WHY?" A strong enough WHY will pull you through every situation and will make you a true conqueror and victor in every occasion. It will lift you far above the average. It makes you go where others stop. It pulls you through the swamps of life when others get stuck, lost or drowned.

I can almost hear what many readers are thinking . . .

"Is this it?"

"How can these words bring all the lofty promises you just made?"

"How can it be that simple?"

"This sounds too simple to be true"

I agree that it's simple, but it's not too simple to be true. In fact, I've learned that most of life's secrets of success are simple.

Goals are great, but a "Why" separates a goal-setter from a goal-achiever and a person that truly changes people's lives!

Too often a "false intellectualism" makes things too complicated to ever succeed.

Yes, it's simply all about the "Why."

The Miracle Inside

You're WHY in life is your biggest, most significant, result-creating force in life. Goals are great, but a "Why" separates a goal-setter from a goal-achiever and a person that truly changes people's lives! Another word that can be used instead of your "Why" is your reason or your purpose.

Your WHY makes all the difference in your life. It separates you from the crowd. A strong WHY will not only make you get up in the morning, but will make you happy, passionate and want to live your life to the fullest!

My goal is for you to "Find Your Why". You will discover that driving force inside of you and feed it with the right words, the right people, the right books, the right motivations and the right inspirational messages. If you do that, then the force – your WHY – will emerge and drive you to success. Do you realize that you have a miracle inside you? We just have to extract it and enable you to fly. As I say, you've got to "Find Your WHY and Fly!"

Let me tell you my story. At the age of 24, I was working seven days a week, more than 12 hours a day, in my family art gallery. My grandfather, whom I truly loved and adored, gave me two of the most powerful values that I still possess today - honesty and hard work.

I graduated as an elite business student from an accredited college, but it got me absolutely nowhere. I respect education, but most of the time education only teaches you about a certain subject. It doesn't train you to achieve success. That is part of what makes my teachings and this book so different. My goal is to train people and motivate them to become successful no matter their level of education, where they came from or any other factor that society uses to determine success. EVERY-ONE can do it!

As you know, I was a stutterer. But, worse than that, I was labeled a stutterer. People would tell me, "John, just stay with your family. That's all you're gonna do. You're gonna work for your family. Don't worry about becoming successful, forget your college degree. You can't even say your name! Who do you think you are? How can you get a regular job? How can you take your college degree and go out and change the world?" I was labeled by society and destined to fail if I listened to them.

If you have been labeled, I want you to tear that label off of you right now! A label is a lie. Labels box people into groups. As I wrote in chapter one, we are not a group. We are individuals. When people called Helen Keller "deaf and dumb", they were labeling her as part of a group of handi-capped people. As a strong individual with a miracle inside, she blew through that group label like a bullet through a bed

> ─── ★ ───
>
> ***"What lies behind us and what lies ahead of us are small matters compared to what lies within us."***
> *- Oliver Wendell Holmes*
>
> ─── ★ ───

sheet. That so-called handicapped lady is one of the most successful people in history.

No one deserves to be labeled no matter the challenges that they face in life. The miracle inside is larger than the label, and inside you are seeds of greatness. The famous and wise Oliver Wendell Holmes said, "What lies behind us and what lies ahead of us are small matters compared to what lies within us".

Learn to Fail Forward

At the age of twenty-four, my life changed when I was introduced to a person that told me, "You can do whatever you want to do in life". I was so excited yet I was scared to death. I couldn't even say my name without stuttering. Could I really do it? How did I meet this person that finally gave me the belief in myself that I had desperately been seeking? I simply answered an ad that said "Make $10,000 a month, wear tailor-made clothes, and drive a Mercedes Benz". I still have the actual phone that I dialed to respond to that ad, because that ad changed my life forever.

I answered the ad and went to an event. The event was on March 15, 1990 at 7:30pm. That night, I was introduced to a business. Most people will be introduced to something that could help them achieve their "Why", but they won't do it. They won't step out in faith or take a risk. In order to succeed in life, you must "fail forward". That's right... fail forward. This means to face your obstacles head on and keep going toward your goal no matter if you succeed or fail. Again, be a full metal jacket. Blow right through obstacles and even the appearance of failure.

Every time you take a risk or you fail forward, you will be a little bit closer to achieving your Why in life.

Don't ever forget this: Every failure is a stepping stone to success, which in turn becomes a very long and lovely stone walkway into the castle of your dreams.

Getting Beyond Security

I was introduced to a vehicle that enabled my "Why" to come to fruition. I listened to a woman speak about a business and a vehicle called Network Marketing. I'll never forget her words. She said, "If you work hard, work smart, and follow a system, you will achieve success."

She also said that I could achieve these three magical words - Time, Freedom and Wealth. That is when I saw the possibility that I, even I, could do what I wanted to do, when I wanted to do it and with who I wanted to do it with. Within seven years of hearing her speak those words of power into my life, I created a very successful business and semi-retired to South Florida.

Yes! I grabbed those words that created the possibility that I could succeed like a drowning man grabbing a life preserver. I said to myself, "I want to empower people. I want to help people realize that they can

If every bill was paid and you had enough money in the bank for the rest of your life, what would you be doing? Take a second and write down your answer.

That is your "Why"!

do whatever they want to do in life". For the first time in my life, I was able to move beyond the comfort zone of security.

I realized that my "security" of working behind the scenes at the art gallery had allowed my stuttering to control me and my life. Security will make you complacent, will control you and will ultimately destroy you. If you're secure right now in your job, then you could be in the process of demolishing your future success. ***Let me ask you a question,*** *if you didn't have to go out and earn money to pay your bills, what would you do? That's right. If every bill was paid and you had enough money in the bank for the rest of your life, what would you be doing? Take a second and write down your answer. Now, that is your "Why"!*

I will come back to that later, but let me tell you what happened when I went home that night from the meeting. I arrived home at my parents' house about 11:30 p.m., and I just started crying. Why? Because I found a way out! I found the actual vehicle that would allow me to achieve my dreams. I could build a business, set myself free and be able to go out and speak to people. I could tell others that it is possible to achieve success, and it is okay to have dreams. That's the night my life and my world changed.

Then, I was introduced to personal development through the classic book, "Think and Grow Rich" by Napoleon Hill. If you don't have that book, then invest in yourself and go buy it. Personal development and the industry of Network Marketing opened my eyes to opportunities that I never knew existed or were possible for even me to achieve.

The next morning as I was driving to the health club at 5:30 a.m., I thought to myself, "I truly don't understand how I'm going to do this. I don't know the business. I don't know the system. I don't know anything." But what I did know was that someone told me I could do it and I was willing to listen to that person.

I was willing to be become success-driven and listen to people that could and would help me become successful and achieve my "Why". To do that meant leaving the comfortable and complacent nest of security. You will never fly, and you will never become a success maniac if you remain in the nest.

Facing Your Fear

About a week into my new business, I attended a seminar. I knew that I would have to stand up and say my name. There I was in a room full of people, labeled a stutterer, sitting in a seminar and listening to people introduce themselves one by one. It was almost my turn, and I walked out of the room. Why? Because I knew I couldn't say my name. I went in the bathroom and sat on the floor and cried. I had convinced myself that there was no way that I could say my name.

What did I do? I remembered my Why, faced my fear and went back inside. I still remember standing up, my knees shaking, heart pounding and sweat coming off me like a waterfall. My eyebrows were even twitching! You know when you're so nervous you can't catch your breath? That's where I was that night. I said, "My name is Ja-Ja-Ja-Ja-Ja-Ja-Ja." I couldn't say my name so I just sat back down in my seat in shame, but that moment was a breakthrough. I vowed that would never happen to me again. As I drove home that day, I said to myself, "No matter what I do, I will never quit!". Guess What? I NEVER DID!

If you have fear in your life, you have to face it, attack it, demolish

*I still remember
standing up,
my knees shaking,
heart pounding
and sweat coming
off me like a
waterfall. My
eyebrows were
even twitching!
You know
when you're
so nervous you
can't catch your
breath?
That's where I
was that night.*

it and pulverize it. I had to do it, and you have to do it. We all have to face our fear in order to achieve our "Why".

Champion, where are you in life? It doesn't matter how far you are from where you want to be in your life. You can produce miracles! I believe you can do it. Do you believe you can do it? Just like I and millions of others, you too can achieve the impossible!

Expect miracles each day. I do. Why not you? YOU CAN DO what you would do if every bill was paid and you had enough money in the bank to last for the rest of your life. You can find out that it is all about the Why.

Many of you reading this book have created a bond with me simply by reading this material. From now on, I want to be your coach, your mastermind team member and your accountability partner.

Are you ready?

Let's go!

CHAPTER FIVE

FINDING YOUR WHY IN LIFE

I told you earlier that I like Champions to take action steps. I have discovered the power of actually standing up, speaking words out loud and writing down specific exercises. Like I wrote earlier, I really do like the Nike advertising line: "Just do it".

Now, we are at the point for you to make one of the most important decisions in life. So, stand up and say this out loud:

"Today, I have started my journey to find my "Why" in life. Life will test me at certain times. But, NO MATTER WHAT, I will complete my journey. At this very moment, I decide I will NEVER quit this journey!"

How does that feel? I know it might have felt a little awkward, but most of you probably felt some type of relief. Remember, what you just shouted out loud is a promise to yourself! Now seal this promise by writing the exact same words that you just said on these lines and Shout it out loud seven times – DO IT NOW!

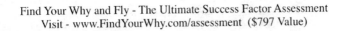

_____

_____

_____

_____

What Does Your "Why" Mean?

Before we start discovering your Why and unleashing your untapped powers and genius, let's take a second to focus on the Why. What is a "Why"? What does it mean? Your "Why" can be defined as your reason or your purpose. It is the reason or purpose that you take up space on this planet.

One of the definitions of "Why" in the Oxford Dictionary is "for what reason or purpose." The same dictionary says this about reason: 1) cause, explanation, or justification; 2) the power of the mind to think, understand and form judgments logically. The same Oxford Dictionary gives one definition of purpose as "the reason for which something is done or something exists". Another word that is frequently used when describing a Why is mission. The Oxford Dictionary refers to the word mission as an assignment.

Whatever term you personally like is up to you. This bit of research will give you some strong references about your "Why" and how to unleash the Champion inside of you. What other words would you use to define your "Why"?

_____

_____

_____

_____

_____

_____

How to Find Your "Why"

Over the years, I've learned that often a person's "Why" is buried down deep inside underneath feelings of doubt and insecurity that have built up like barnacles on a bottom of a ship. The good news is that we – YOU – can and will extract your Why. By harnessing courage, you can confidently go to the next level in your life. As I told you, my goal is to assist you "Find Your Why" no matter how deep it's hidden inside you and no matter how much negativity we have to scrape off the top of it.

In order to help you "Find Your Why", let me tell you some more of my story as well as some other electrifying testimonials. The power of this story will inspire you and help you discover your Why in life. It will also ignite a burning desire within your guts to start digging and polishing your "Why".

You will see, understand, discover and feel that your "Why" is the #1 factor that determines all your successes and failures for the rest of your life. That's right. Your "Why" is the Ultimate Success Factor. Let me tell you that I am committed to give you all that I have in order to motivate and inspire you to achieve your "Why". *In life, your mind might choose your profession,*

Let your heart out of its cage. Release your heart to dream about an unimaginable future. Don't you owe that to yourself? Is the rest of your life important enough to make this investment in yourself?

your hobbies, or the way you spend your leisure time. But, your heart chooses your "Why".

I'm asking you stop rushing your life for a few moments and make room in your heart for that spark to ignite. Let your heart out of its cage. Release your heart to dream about a unimaginable future. Don't you owe that to yourself? Is the rest of your life important enough to make this investment in yourself? You need to write down your thoughts and expand on them. You have got to be open to receive.

Even as a stutterer, I knew my Why was to change people's lives. When I went out to that seminar, I didn't see just a business. I saw a vehicle that would allow me to attain my "Why". I saw a vehicle, a means of transportation, that would empower me to set goals and achieve financial freedom so I could achieve my Why.

Let me ask you, "Have you thought about what vehicle will carry you into achieving your Why?" Do you know what it is? Some of you may know, and some of you may still be searching. That's fine. Just begin to daydream about it. Daydreaming is the best and most dynamic part of a true champion's day. Write down your vehicle or vehicles that will assist you in achieving your Why in life.

_____

_____

_____

_____

_____

_____

_____

Now ask yourself, "What is my Why?" What is your passion, your purpose and your ultimate goal in life? What would you do if you had all the money and time that you ever needed. Let your heart soar and write down your thoughts on the lines below. If you run out of space, grab another piece of paper and keep on writing. Let your future flow through your pen. Do not edit or correct it YET, just keep on writing. Let it flow from your heart! (Let the Emotion really flow because it will create Massive Movement – GO for it – Right NOW!)

_____

_____

_____

_____

_____

_____

_____

_____

_____

_____

_____

_____

_____

_____

_____

Your "Why" must be bigger than who you are right now. Remember, the "Why" is your ultimate dream, goal and desire in life. If you are having some difficulty discovering or writing your "Why", then here's one of my student's Why Cards as an example.

My Why is...

"The reason I am dealing with all the challenges of building my business today is because my 'Why' is to be financially secure so that I may spend quality time with my wife and children. I actually see us traveling together as a family to many cities and countries around the world. I also see my children duplicating the success that I have in my business. They are empowering others to pursue their dreams and succeed. They are making a difference in the world today. Having this financial freedom will allow me to touch the lives of those in need, especially those children who have no parents, those who were stripped of all their hopes, dreams and left to the streets or orphanages. Sixty percent of my income and time will be directed to specific ministries that will provide education, give food, shelter and love to these children. I also donate 30% of my earnings to my church."

That's a very powerful Why Card, but the first day that I sat with this individual he didn't say all of that. I had him write down the three magical words: "My Why is". He took those three words home and let his heart do the rest, and that is how he ultimately wrote the magnificent "Why" you just read. After he wrote his Why and internalized it, his business grew threefold.

Now we have expanded on developing a "Why", let's dig a little deeper in your own Why in life. Let's crystallize your initial thoughts a little more by rewriting your Why. That's right, do it again and write from your heart.

My Why is...(Most Important 3 words)

_____

_____

_____

_____

_____

_____

_____

_____

_____

_____

_____

_____

_____

_____

_____

_____

_____

——— ⭐ ———

A genuine "Why" should scare you a little bit! The sheer possibilities of it should blow your socks off.

——— ⭐ ———

Once again, your Why must be bigger than who you are right now. In fact, I will let you in on a little secret. You should think so big that it actually scares you into success. That's right. A genuine "Why" should scare you a little bit! The sheer possibilities of it should blow your socks off. I remember the title of an old novel, "Sometimes a Great Notion". A true Why captures the possibilities of what happens when "sometimes a great notion" seizes your heart. When it seizes your heart, it takes over. It will drive you! That's part of the secret of Rick Warren's phenomenally successful book, "The Purpose-Driven Life". Your purpose (Your Why) will drive you.

A true Why will ignite you and fuel your dreams. Your Why will change your daily actions and drive you to places you have never seen or considered before. Your Why will pull you through the ditches and dirt of life. It will set you apart from the crowd. It will give you that little bit of extra that makes you happy, passionate, proud and prosperous in all areas in your life.

I know there is a WHY in you! It might be covered by a layer of unproductive programming, and you might not feel worthy of achieving anything greater than what you are right now. That's okay. Don't worry about it. Things will begin to change, because you have ignited a powerful spark inside of your heart. You did it by simply writing out your

"Why".

It's like a seed that has fallen into the soil. It will take on a life of its own. You don't have to keep digging it up to see if it's growing. All you need to do is give it some time. This moment, later today or tomorrow, find a place where you feel comfortable and open up this book again. Start reading it from the very first page. Take your time to ponder, think and write. Take your time to feel the spark. Finally, write down the three magic words, "My Why is". Write it all out again. Write it as though it's the first time. No, it's not redundant. ***It's an action step on your road to success. It's recommended by your coach, mastermind team member, and accountability partner . . . ME!*** I promise you that when you follow these exact steps, your spark will ignite and you will be on fire for your life and your Why.

For years, and probably decades, you've been beat up by negative words in every part of your life. What words? Well, do any of these sound familiar?

"You can't do it!"

"Who do you think you are?"

"You're nothing special!"

"Don't you know where you came from?"

"Who are you trying to kid?"

"Remember when you failed at..."

Erase those words from your memory and vocabulary. I am telling you that YOU CAN DO IT! Whatever lingers deep inside you, YOU CAN DO IT! Remember, I couldn't speak fluently for the first twenty-four years of my life. I was told to stop trying, because I "can't even talk". I was doubted by almost everyone in my life based on the label that was stuck on my forehead by society. Does this sound familiar to you?

I couldn't speak fluently, but my "Why" was big enough and strong enough to pull me through the impossible. Every day I stood there by the Hudson River, screaming letter for letter the entire alphabet. *My miracle happened one letter at a time. I did it and so can you!*

Your birth certificate (Certificate of Life) gives you the right to go out and achieve all your goals, dreams and desires in life. Remember, we all start on equal ground with our birth certificate, but it is up to you to make your life different from the average, normal person that just settles for what they are handed in life or for whatever security that have found that protects them from facing their fears. "Find your Why and Fly!"

CHAPTER SIX

UNLEASHING YOUR WHY IN LIFE

By now, I'm sure you're well on the way to finding or perhaps you have already found that spark inside your heart. That spark is what ignites that roaring fire of desire deep inside of you. I salute you! You're doing something that most people never achieve. You're discovering your ultimate Why in life. Writing your "Why" is a process, and you can rewrite it as many times as you need in the beginning phase. Every great accomplishment starts with one step towards its achievement.

The Incredible Power of a 3x5 Card

There is one more secret that I have to tell you before we move on talking about the Why. You might want to know why I haven't talked about "how" you can achieve your "Why" yet. Your success is 95% from your "Why" and only 5% comes from the actual "How" you will accomplish it. In other words, don't worry so much about the "How" just keep focusing on the "Why" at this point. My own experience is that if your Why is strong enough, then you will never have to worry about the How. Strangely enough, the "How" will present itself. I've seen it happen many times.

Now, let's talk about the real power behind your Why. The way for you to unleash the true power behind your Why is simple. Grab a 3x5 index card. I'm gonna say that once again. Grab a 3x5 index card. This is a million dollar tool, but it is so simple that most people won't do it! You could have expensive software that would allow you to create a fancy, multi-colored, seven-dimension, micro-chip implanted "Why" card. You could have everything under the sun, but this little 3x5 index card will change your life. It will massively change your life!

Start internalizing your "Why" in your mind, your heart and your spirit. It will change your life forever, and you will never go back to that point you were at before you found your "Why".

At the top of the index card write "My Why Card" in big letters. Then, write your personal Why statement on this card beginning with "My Why is". After you've done that, you must commit to reading it over and over and over again! The power of the "Why Card" lies in its mobility. You can take it everywhere you go, and you will never lose focus on the achievement of your Why.

With every challenge or obstacle in life that you face, simply face it head on and READ YOUR WHY CARD. Start internalizing your "Why" in your mind, your heart and your spirit. It will change your life forever, and you will never go back to that point you were at before you found your "Why".

The First Seven Minutes of Each Day

OK, Listen up.. this is your coach speaking. One of the most important daily action steps is that you read your Why Card for the first seven minutes of your day. It is of the highest importance that you spend the first seven minutes upon arising every day reading your Why card. That's right. You MUST read your Why Card every morning when you get up. It's called the "Why Rollover". Rollover, grab your Why card and read it!

Imagine reading your Why Card the first seven minutes of your day instead of picking up your cell phone, checking your email, and clicking on television to watch everything bad that is happening in the world. Isn't your Why more important to you than those things? Start internalizing your Why. Start meditating on it for seven minutes early in the morning when you get up. This meditation period will set your day on fire! It will add a snap to your step and a smile to your face, because you know your Why. You know why you do what you do every single day and that you will ultimately achieve your Why in life.

Write this down and say it out loud:

"I have decided that I will read my Why Card every morning for the first seven minutes and that I will do so immediately upon rising. I will internalize my Why and feel my heart grow full of joy, excitement, determination, and creativity every day because I know my Why!"

_____

_____

_____

_____

_____

The Last Thing Every Night

What's the next step? Let me give you another Million Dollar Tip that will catapult your belief in your Why. Here it is. Read your Why Card before going to bed and meditate on it for a few moments. Go over the day and ask yourself, "What did I do today that will assist me in the achievement of my Why?" Then ask yourself, "What can I do tomorrow to improve my daily championship action steps that will ultimately lead to the achievement of my Why?"

Write all these things down in your personal Why journal. Just like the 3x5 Index Card, use a basic notebook for your Why Journal. A Why Journal is a tool that you can keep on your night stand or near your bed. Every night, jot down your answers to these two questions:

1. "What did I do today that will assist me in the achievement of my Why?"
2. "What can I do tomorrow to improve my daily championship action steps that will ultimately lead to the achievement of my Why?"

These Champion habits will pulverize old and unproductive behaviors. These habits will increase your success pace drastically! I know many of you are saying to yourself, "But, I don't have time to read the Why Card in the morning and at night". *Let me ask you a heart-wrenching question,* *"Are you committed to achieving your Why in life?"* If so, then you will soon realize that the amount of time you invest reading your Why Card every morning and every night will determine when and if you achieve your Why in life.

The Purpose of Problems

The number of obstacles that you face in life will lay the foundation for massive growth. One of the most important principles to under-stand as you build your future is that *problems have a purpose*. A wise man once said, "The doorway to success is camouflaged by problems". That's why there are challenges, obstacles and hurdles between you and success.

That's the reason I often say and even wrote in the introduction to this book that my stuttering handicap turned into a pre-cious gift in my life. It became the driving force behind me creating the most powerful success key of "Find Your Why". Success is always hidden by challenges and prob-lems. In solving them, you acquire skills

The ultimate success is always hidden by problems. In solving them, you acquire skills that you need to be a leader.

that you need to be a leader. Just as the butterfly must struggle to shed its cocoon, we all have to struggle to climb out of failure and into success. In fighting its way out of the cocoon, the butterfly develops muscles that it will need to fly. I once heard a man describe trying to help a butterfly get free of its cocoon. He took a knife and cut the cocoon away. The butterfly came out, but then died right before his eyes! That butterfly needed – and we all need – the struggle to achieve.

The great Russian novelist Aleksandr Solzhenitsyn once said, "Even biology teaches us that habitual well-being is not favorable to life". We all need to struggle our way into success. Striving to succeed will always be part of achieving your Why. When we don't have struggles or obstacles to overcome, we become complacent, lazy and passive.

My coaching student that wrote the "Why" statement that you read

You must SEE yourself achieving your Why. That's why many successful sports trainers make their students visualize the golf ball rolling into the cup, the basketball swooshing the net, the arrow hitting the core of the target. If you see it, you can do it.

earlier certainly understands that concept. That's the reason he began his Why by saying, "The reason why I am dealing with all the challenges. . . " He didn't flinch at the possibility of obstacles. He embraced them. Just settle it in your mind that you will have challenges, you will have obstacles and you will have hurdles—no question about it!

That same champion student also uses the words, "I actually see..." This is a critically important key to the process of overcoming the problems. You must SEE yourself successful, and you must SEE yourself achieving your Why. That's why many successful sports trainers make their students visualize the golf ball rolling into the cup, the basketball swooshing the net, the arrow hitting the core of the target, etc. If you see it, you can do it. *If you can't see yourself (visualize) achieving your Why, then your belief in your Why is not strong enough.*

The discovery of your Why is a great milestone in your life. You will change, and you will improve yourself. Your interests will change, and you will expand. You will enjoy life even more than you already do. In order for this to happen, you must invest in yourself, face the problems and see yourself achieving your Why.

CHAPTER SEVEN

THE GROWING WHY

Your Why is a burning desire. It drives you to achieve your ultimate goals in life. As your life progresses and your horizons expand, your Why will also naturally progress. Here's an important principle: *Your Why Expands As You Grow.*

With your "Why" growing and expanding, it is very likely you will notice more changes in your life. All of the sudden, you change your habits and you are more interested in investing more time in your personal development. Personal development is the key to advancing yourself mentally, physically and socially in order to achieve your Why.

The Power of Other People

As your "Why" expands and becomes more developed, you will find yourself growing past some old friends and your current lifestyle. Just visualize adding a drop of water to a glass everyday. Soon the glass will overflow, and you will need a bigger glass. It's the same as your Why. You will out grow the everyday normalcy, your Why will start spilling over into every part of your life and you will start to reach for bigger and better things.

It may be painful or difficult, but creating change in your life always provokes change in your friends. It often takes courage and resolve to make those changes especially when it means that you must leave behind people that you have known all of your life. Many times, those same people just fall away when they see the "new you". However it happens, change will always bring new friends and lose some old ones.

One of the principles in Napoleon Hill's "Think and Grow Rich" is let great people shape your life. That principle will always carry us away from people who are not great and will only keep us from achieving our Why. It is very likely that you will decide to just stop associating with certain people in your life. Some people have the unfortunate power to disconnect us from achieving our Why; therefore, we must make the decision to stop allowing those people to squash our dreams.

An accomplished and successful musician once said, "Critics are only remembered for what they failed to understand." Don't allow the critics to kill your dream. Too many people have lost their dreams, because they have surrendered to the challenges that life threw at them. Those same challenges are often thrown by people that don't understand their own music in their heart.

Many champions that disconnect themselves from the critics find themselves entering into a lonely, isolation zone. This is normal. It's just part of the "friend exchange" that goes with your new life. You must be determined to surround yourself with other Champions that believe in you and want you to succeed by developing a Mastermind Team.

Your Mastermind Team should consist of people that will walk with you on your path to success. They are people that will encourage you as you face challenges that threaten your ultimate achievement of your Why. Do you have a Mastermind Team? Let's see. Write down the top five people that you associate with on a daily basis (please be truthful).

1. _____

2. _____

3. _____

4. _____

5. _____

Now, cross off those people that are hindering and holding back your success. These are the critics that simply can't understand your music (your Why). They refuse to believe that you can and will do better things with your life. Don't be surprised if you are left with only one or zero people out of those five. I've seen so many people give up on their dreams and the achievement of their Why, because they simply didn't have a Mastermind Team to support them.

The Motivational Club

It's very frustrating for me to see Champions fail because of their everyday associations with naysayers. That's why I along with my team decided to take action and create the Motivational Club. This Club is the hottest Club of Champions you can imagine. Every month we'll send *YOU* a motivational CD and a DVD, and you will also have ultimate access

───── ⭐ ─────

The Motivational Club is the hottest club of champions that you can imagine.

───── ⭐ ─────

to prerecorded Monday Night Millionaire Motivational LIVE Tele-Classes. Above and beyond all of that, there is an interactive Champions forum, where you can actively network and associate with Champions all over the world.

I believe this club is a MUST for dream builders. Why? As I said before, it is very hard to achieve your Why by yourself. You need a support system...someone that believes in you. Start building your Mastermind Team today by visiting www.FindYourWhy.com/club. Find out how you can build your own Mastermind Team of Champions!!!

By changing your actions in life, you will change your results. By changing your results, you will notice that the quality of your life improves. This all happens, because you took the time and effort to find and ultimately achieve your Why in life.

Write down five action steps that you are committed to taking in pursuit of the achievement of your Why.

_____

_____

_____

_____

_____

CHAPTER EIGHT

INFECT OTHERS WITH SUCCESS

Do you remember the principle of sowing and reaping? This is an important key to success. You can soar to unparalleled heights in your life, and part of what carries you there is the power of sowing the right kind of seed. Learn to share, influence and improve the lives of others. Basically, if you want to change your life radically, make sure that you commit yourself to assisting others and leading by example.

As I said before, there is no better exercise than reaching down and lifting someone up. We all have a need to help others and to give back some of what we've been given. When you read the "Why" statements of Champions, you will see that golden thread running through everything they envision for a successful future.

For example, when I first went out to the bookstore to pick up "Think and Grow Rich", I proudly showed it to everyone around me. I told them that if Napoleon Hill's son could be cured of deafness, then I would be a fluent speaker. Although this seemed impossible *(always remember inside the word impossible is possible)*, it excited me to share (sow this seed) with my friends and family. Sharing makes you bigger and makes you accountable to yourself and others.

Don't be afraid to share your feelings and don't be afraid of one or two negative reactions. Most people think negative and will respond to

———— ★ ————

*Tell them
they need
to start by
finding their
"Why"
and then
actively
pursuing it.*

———— ★ ————

your dream of achieving your Why with negativity. You must continue to tell your friends and family about your Why and your longing to better yourself and your life.

Tell them that you feel that they also can achieve miracles in life. Tell them they need to start by finding their "Why" and then actively pursuing it.

From that point, follow-up with them about their progress and share your progress with them. This will show them how much you care about them, but it will also assist you in the ultimate achievement of your "Why". Why? Because you are sowing seeds into the lives of others and you will reap a bountiful harvest.

Lead by example. After you share your Why with others, they will watch you a little closer. They will notice that you are changing. They will see that you enjoy life more and that you are achieving massive results. This will inspire them to ask you, "What has happened with you?" This is simply positive reinforcement that will assist you to face the challenges that life throws at you and achieve your Why. I want to see success spread like a prairie fire across the world. My personal dream is to see millions connect with their own personal "Why" and achieve success beyond their dreams.

Now, create a plan of action that includes you sharing your "Why" with others and describe how your Why will impact their lives. Go ahead, take action now!

CHAPTER NINE

MORE MAGIC BEHIND THE WHY

I want to share a real-life example with you. One of my students catapulted his life to new levels, because he discovered and applied the true power behind the "Why". Now, I am going to breakdown his "Why" so you can feel and find the power behind it.

First, he wrote "**MY WHY IS . . .** *I am a home-based entrepreneur because I am an optimistic maverick at heart. While I am a team player, I feel passionate about being responsible for my own growth and happiness rather than dealing with a coarse and cutting senior manager controlling my destiny. I do not care to be dependent on some company's time schedule, budget, or benefit plan.*"

This is great stuff! He is announcing who he is, what he's passionate about and even what he hates. He doesn't want to deal with certain influences and limitations anymore. You can tell that he despises it (hate can be a very passionate and positive emotion).

He goes on to say, "*Every day, I will listen to 50 minutes of coaching tapes and read personal development and leadership books . . . 50 minutes a day to become more efficient and more effective.*"

This man is so focused! He is making a deliberate choice to only "eat" and digest the right mental foods. He's saying that what he listens to is important. If he listens to junk, he'll become junk. If he listens to successful coaches, then he will become successful.

Then he writes, *"My vision for 2012 is to be healthy, free and committed to helping create 1,000 millionaires. My vision is to help 1,000 freedom-orientated people to become life-style freedom coaches and millionaires. Yes! I will help create 1,000 millionaires in my lifetime."*

If your "Why" is not so big that it changes who you are, then it's not big enough!

Very powerful and very focused. Once again, he's speaking his "Why" forward. It's more than feelings or vague desires. He is speaking activity. He is speaking "Why" words. His Why is bigger than who he is! Remember, your Why must be bigger than who you are. It must change the person that you are. If your Why is not so big that it changes who you are, it's not big enough. I'll repeat that again, If your Why is not so big that it changes who you are, then it's not big enough!

Now, I want you to break down your Why like I did with the Why above. You must know and understand your Why inside and out. Your Why is the foundation of your success in life and must be rock solid.

Break down your Why. Use a separate sheet of paper if you need it.

_____

_____

_____

_____

There are three major obstacles that will hinder your achievement of your "Why" if you don't take action. As we progress through these obstacles, I'm going to bring you back to times that life threw these same three major obstacles at me to distract me from achieving my Why life.

What are the Obstacles?

I told you there would be obstacles. As you know, my main obstacle was stuttering. Remember, these obstacles and problems actually serve a purpose in achieving your Why. What are they? ***The first obstacle that will hinder the achievement of your Why is "toxic" people around you.*** These people will tell you things like, "Are you crazy?" "Who do you think you are?" "You're not going to build a business!" "You're not going to earn that kind of money!" "You're not going to become financially free!"

That's why I call them "toxic people". They will poison your success journey. Do not let negativity just ooze onto your doorstep! Here's what I've learned. Love your friends that do not support you moving to the next level in life, but make a decision today to move on from them. Of course you love them, but you have to love yourself enough to leave them and stop them from stealing your dreams.

Remember this: *leaving them is also an act of love. Go "Find Your Why", accomplish your dreams and then come back later to share your success with them. In other words, when you have the strength and the strong foundation of life, you can reach out to them. This is a simple technique called love them, leave them and show them.*

Do you ever notice that when flight attendants prepare the passengers for the flight they talk about the oxygen mask? They say, "In the event of a sudden cabin depressurization, oxygen masks will drop down. Please secure your own mask before helping others." That's not selfish! If you don't guarantee your own oxygen flow, then you won't have the strength or consciousness to help anyone else. In the same sense, go work on your own dream. When you've done all of that and are successful, you can go back and help those who tried to kill your dream.

The second obstacle that will hinder the achievement of your "Why" are the chains shackled to your ankles. Let's talk about those chains. Most of them are composed of your P-A-S-T. Everyone has experienced failure. Everyone has made mistakes. Everyone has done stupid things. The past can only hold power over your future IF YOU LET IT! That's right. Your past will haunt you for the rest of your life if you let it. It will drag you back to the place that you were before you found your Why. It will also prevent you from moving forward towards the achievement of your Why. You have to ask yourself an honest question and more importantly answer it. Are you letting the chains of your past hold you down? If so, I suggest you look down, take the chains, throw them away and never look down again.

Harriet Tubman is known for abolishing slavery in the United States and was once quoted as saying, "I freed thousands of slaves and could have freed thousands more if they only knew that they were slaves". This great quote applies to life in general. Many times, we simply don't know what is holding us back; therefore, we are unable to take the action needed to create massive success in our lives. You must be aware of what is preventing you from gaining freedom in all areas of your life before you can ultimately achieve your Why.

The third obstacle that will hinder the achievement of your "Why"
is – Giving UP! It is easy to give up and say to yourself, "This is not
gonna work! I can't do it! I quit!" Many years ago, I remember opening
the door to the Rye Town Hilton. I walked up the stairs to the meeting
room and saw a sign-in table. Immediately, the little inner voice said,
"Ha Ha! You gotta say your name! Go back to the art gallery. No way,
loser...stutterer...fool! What are you doing out here? Just go home. Go
home, eat, watch tv, go to bed, wake up...just like you did for twenty-
four years. Go work at the art gallery."

But I stepped out in faith! I didn't know back then what faith was
or how to take a risk. I simply had no clue, but I didn't give up on
my dreams. As I progressed towards the table, I saw a sign-in sheet.
I looked down and the man at the table said "What is your name?" I
grabbed a blue tag and I wrote my name down. I flipped it around, and
he read it. He said, "Oh, Hi John!" I said "Hi!" Why? I was too afraid
to say my own name, because I knew that I would stutter.

I am now an international motivational speaker, inspirational writ-
er, a mentor to millionaires and a strategic business coach. How is this
possible for a stuttering fool? I knew my Why and I did not quit! I say
that with full conviction and confidence, because I know that you can
do the same. Right now, I want you to write down these words and internalize them.

Failure and Quitting are NOT Options!

In order to achieve your Why, you must have those words instilled
in your spirit and believe that you will succeed no matter what.

Live *Monday Night Motivational* Tele Class 8:30 p.m. EST.
Dial: 212-990-8000 - Access Code: 7458# - ($497 Value)

CHAPTER TEN

A VIEW FROM THE MOUNTAIN

When we discover new and life-altering truths, we are like pioneers standing on a mountain ridge looking at a new beginning. In the cool, crisp morning air, we can see forever. Then, our gaze slowly and finally settles on a beautiful valley. The vivid colors of the grass and lakes and the framing horizons of sky and mountain peaks are just breathtaking. In that golden moment, our heart says, "Yes. That's it! That's where I want to spend the rest of my life". We can hardly wait to get down there and go to work building the future. Our heart almost explodes as we imagine breaking the sod, planting crops, building a house and joining with other like-minded people in creating a new community. We are seized by "Sometimes a Great Notion".

We finally arrive in that valley and begin to carve out that new life. At first, it's romantic and exciting, but after a while reality sets in. We discover that it's too hot in the summer and too cold in the winter. Mosquitoes, crickets and rattlesnakes can make life difficult. When we initially saw the gorgeous and lush green meadow from the mountain top, we didn't realize that much of the green was weeds. At that point, the faint-hearted will become discouraged and begin gazing at the next mountain range. They end up forsaking the valley in pursuit of another dream. Too many remain wanderers in life drifting away from the dream and always preoccupied by new mountain ridges.

For example, some people are like that regarding their own marriage. They begin in great excitement, romance and passion. But when they get into the hard work and heavy lifting of building a life with another person, they get discouraged and start looking for someone else.

Refresh Your Vision

> *... when discouragement sets in, it's best to go back to the mountain top where you stood the first time that your eyes fell on the "valley". Refresh your vision! Remind yourself of the great possibilities that you once saw.*

I've learned that when discouragement sets in, it's best to go back to the mountain top where you stood the first time your eyes fell on the "valley". Refresh your vision! Remind yourself of the great possibilities that you once saw. For example, go back in your mind to when you first saw your husband or wife. What was it that you saw in her/him? Remember the way that your spouse held his/her head and smiled as he/she listened to you talk. Remember how he/she laughed when you told a joke. Remember how his/her eyes filled with tears when he/she saw you coming down the aisle of the church on your wedding day.

Sometimes, we just have to go back and revisit the view and refresh the vision that we had from the mountain. That applies to our "Why" as well as to our spouse. No matter what, your "Why" is still there as radiant and full of possibilities as ever. You just have to refresh your vision of what you saw the first time that you ever imagined it or wrote out your Why Card.

In this last chapter, I want to take you back to the mountain and refresh your vision of what you saw when you first read it. *I recommend that you reread this chapter (return to the mountain) once a week until it's inscribed in your heart and mind.*

Let's take a few minutes to climb back up to the peak from which you first saw the possibilities of a new life. Here are some of the things you saw:

Find Your Why and Fly!

I want to break this down word by word so you can get a renewed vision for it.

- *"Find"*

  You have to FIND it. Your "Why" will not seek you out. It will not hunt you down and wrap itself around your life. You have to dig, search, excavate and often get frustrated or even angry as you work to FIND it. Olympians spend years practicing and training for the Olympics prior to ever attending the actual events. They are laser-focused on winning a gold medal. You have to display the same kind of tenacious, relentless and patient focus on FINDING your why.

- *"Your"*

  We're working on YOUR Why not mine or anyone else. You are responsible for it, not me, not your mother, not your boss, not the President. You own it.

If your "Why" doesn't fit, if it doesn't challenge you, if it doesn't capture your own dream, YOU are the one who has to fix it, adjust it, change it, modify it.

• *"Why"*

This is the core, the center, of your life. It is the driving force, and the very reason why you even take up space on the planet. Your "Why" is your reason for living, your great and compelling purpose. If it doesn't scare you, it's too small. If it doesn't change you, it's an insufficient "Why."

• *"And"*

The very simple word "and" is a very important conjunction. According to Webster's New World Dictionary "and" means "next" or "thereupon" or "in addition to". In other words, Finding Your Why leads to something else. "And" also establishes the order. In this case, you have to "Find Your Why" and only THEN can you Fly! If you try to fly first, then you will end up flat on your face because you haven't learned to use your wings.

• *"Fly"*

Jim Rohn talks about "living where you want to live, wearing what you want to wear and driving what you want to drive". In other words, a vital part of life is getting to taste the sweet fruit of success. "Finding Your Why" leads to Flying. Of course, you can't do this part first. The fruit, the result and the outcome of Finding Your Why is the ability to Fly beyond all of your hopes and dreams. You will finally understand what success feels like.

Here are some other things you saw from the mountain ridge:

Reclaim Your Birthright

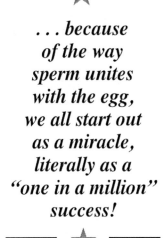

... because of the way sperm unites with the egg, we all start out as a miracle, literally as a "one in a million" success!

Never forget that the most important day of your life is your birthday. That's why the day is special. That's why you (and those who love you) celebrate it. It's more than just a cultural thing. We have a sense down deep in our heart that the day is significant.

Why? First off, because of the way sperm unites with the egg, we all start out as a miracle, literally as a "one in a million" success! At birth, we all start out the same. We're on the same planet, we're subject to the same natural laws, and we all start out in the womb as a miracle of success.

That's also why our birth certificate is so important. It is a legal document that gives you the right to grow up and become a Champion. That piece of paper is your "Certificate of Life". Unlike working for a college degree, you automatically earn your Certificate of Life when you exit the womb. No questions asked . . . you are destined for success.

Refuse to Be a Victim

Our society carries a relentless temptation to blame someone else. Victimization is the ethic of our times. It has a way of becoming our work ethic (the boss or the company are the reason we don't succeed), our marriage ethic (our spouse keeps us from becoming who we were meant to be) and our life ethic (because my mother or father or 3rd grade teacher damaged me with their insults, I will never be a whole person).

When we break the cycle of blame, we take responsibility for our own life. It is only when we decide to stop blaming others that we begin to succeed.

Reprogram Your Computer

Our life's default program is one of discouragement, temptation, fear, anger and doubt. It projects discouraging, dangerous and defeating messages. This default program comes mostly from television, newspapers, music, movies, billboards and real live people. All of us walk through a daily bombardment of programmed words that are highly toxic.

Here's the process by which the default programming is installed on our internal computer. What comes in our ears, enters into our heart and then comes out our mouth. ***Ears > Heart > Mouth***. Even Jesus said we are defiled by what comes out of our mouth. Just further proving that this is not a new concept.

We have to reprogram our internal computer. We have to deliberately choose the "software" that will make it run clean, smooth and fast. That software is a combination of the words that we read and the words that we hear. These words form the "software" attitudes, thoughts and expectations of our life. Therefore, we must be careful what we watch and read. Words are some of the most powerful things in life. They are seeds. When these seeds fall into the soil of our lives, they take on a life of their own. The seeds start to develop roots, take over the field and create a massive crop. That's why we have to be vigilant even militant to only sow the right kind of seeds.

I rarely watch TV. Why? Because it's like inviting a negative, lying, cynical and flirtatious person to live in my house. Why would I do that? Why would I invite someone I didn't trust or even like to live in my house? I'm always amazed when I hear parents talk about having to "monitor" the TV for their kids. Would they invite a dangerous, crazy person to live in their house and then feel the need to be present every time he/she talked to their kids? NO! Not only would you NOT invite someone like that to live in your house, but you would get a restraining order to keep them far away from your house and your kids.

. . . we have to reprogram our internal computer. We have to deliberately choose the "software" which will make it run clean, smooth, and fast. That software is a combination of the words we read and the words we hear.

The reason I'm writing so much about TV is that in our society television is one of the biggest source of "programming" that goes on in our internal computer. There is no need to monitor TV programs for your family. It's simple. Don't allow the garbage to enter your home and poison the minds of your family.

————— ★ —————

Forget the Past

*. . . one thing
I do: forgetting
what lies behind
and reaching
forward to what
lies ahead,
I press on
toward the goal
for the prize
of the
upward call. . .*
– Philippians 3:13-14

————— ★ —————

All of us have made mistakes, committed sins, disappointed our family and friends, and even injured other people. Those things can be haunting, but all that we can do is to try to make things right with people and move on.

Most of us also have great successes in our past, and sometimes the successes are as restricting as the failures. When we have an image of something we accomplished, that image often has a way of blinding us from seeing the brand-new possibilities that may be different and better than what we've already attained.

For some reason, we have trouble escaping our past failures and successes. As long as we are a prisoner to the past, we can never fully embrace the new future that awaits us.

That's why one of the greatest figures in world history, the Apostle Paul, said, ". . . one thing I do: forgetting what lies behind and reaching forward to what lies ahead, I press on toward the goal for the prize of the upward call. . ." (Philippians 3:13-14). Our past has no hold on us. It can only hurt or be an obstacle if we allow that in our mind. That's the lesson of "kicking the chicken". Let me refresh your memory. When farmers take chickens to the market, they will often tie their ankles and lay them in the bed of their truck for the ride to the sale barn. This prevents them from flying out of the truck.

When they arrive at the sale barn, he will take them out of the truck, place them on the ground, and then cut the cords, releasing them to get up. But, the chickens won't get up! They think they're still bound at their ankles, so they just lay there. The farmer has to actually kick them to stir them to flutter and get up. Sometimes, we must "kick the chicken" in ourselves in order to get out of our obsession with our imprisonment to our past. So, "kick the chicken" in yourself. Your ankles are free! Get up and walk around. Celebrate your freedom.

Discover the Power of Commitment

Commitment is the foundation for building your life. It is the bedrock of achieving your ultimate "Why" in life. Commitment is that hammer-hard, "burn-the-boats", full-speed-ahead determination to do, to be and to achieve something. Nothing, absolutely nothing will stop a person of genuine commitment.

One of the main reasons that Champions have commitment is to just get through the clutter, the confusion and the noise in our society. We are saturated with lights, colors and voices. It's so easy to just flop down and watch TV or go to

. . . every success maniac should commit to regularly scheduling time with a good book or a conversation with his or her spouse or quality time with his or her children. It is also important to schedule time with other Champions . . .

the mall or hang out at the local pub. To really focus on achieving massive results requires a very serious commitment to our own future. Do you have that kind of commitment?

For example, do you make appointments with yourself? Do you make them with your own spouse and children? A genuine depth of commitment will cause you to take your own life and your family seriously. We schedule time for meetings with our business associates, beauticians, bankers and others that are far less important to us than our own future and our family members. Perhaps our priorities need to be remodeled.

Every champion, every success maniac, should commit to regularly scheduling time with a good book or a conversation with his/her spouse or quality time with his/her children. It is also important to schedule time with other Champions. Let them infect you with their success and winning attitude.

Build a Habit of Giving Generously

If you knew that all healthy people had one thing in common, wouldn't you want to know that one health secret? Well, if you want to be magnificently successful, you need to know the one victory secret that Champions have in common. That one thing is the habit of generous giving.

Giving is an attitude. It finds real and deep joy in blessing other people. To give generously is to discover a secret fountain in the heart and when you give your life away, it always returns to you in fuller, deeper, richer measure than it was when you gave it away. Sowing and reaping are principles of the universe. Whatever and however you sow is the same measure by which you will reap. Take that to the bank!

Embrace the Miracle

Every person in the world is unique. There are no two people alike, and every person is a miracle. Just the fact that you were born means that you have already achieved against great odds.

We are all caught in a war. Part of the war is the chorus of voices that try to devalue your uniqueness and steal your dream. The voices all try to make us part of a group. A major part of embracing and celebrating the miracle is to reject the label. Always remember that you are YOU! You are not a group.

Keep Moving Past the Obstacles

The three main obstacles standing between you and success are:

1. Toxic People
2. Your Past
3. Giving Up

Set your face toward your future and move right on past those obstacles. Do not be distracted by anything or anyone. It's YOUR life. Don't stop or take a detour. Remain focused on the goal and keep moving.

The Bible tells the story of Jesus healing a paralyzed man. What

Jesus said is very instructive for us, "Rise, take up your bed, and walk". I think he may have told him to pick up his bed in order to remove the temptation of falling back into bed! Once you pick up your bed, it's easier to remain focused on walking. As long as the bed beckons, we're always tempted to quit.

Face Your Fear

Fear is no stranger to me. I've told you my story of stuttering, but you have a story of fear too. In fact, everyone reading this book knows fear. Most people assume that they have some special fear. That's simply not true. Your fear may be slightly different than mine, but fear is universal. Everyone has it, and everyone has to choose how to deal with it.

If you are going to achieve greatness and if you are going to be a champion, you first have to face, attack, demolish and pulverize fear. I had to do it. You have to do it. We all have to face our fear in order to achieve our "Why". Don't let fear intimidate you. Remember that everyone that ever lived had to deal with fear. You can and will do it!

"Why" is More Important than "How"

Having a strong and focused north star of purpose is vastly more important than knowing HOW you're going to achieve that purpose. The "Why" will give birth to the How. If you focus on the How, then you'll never have a large enough "Why".

Sometimes I think the news media has turned us into "how addicts".

You've heard it all. . . "How will you do that, Mr. President?" "How can we ever solve a global crisis like AIDS?" "Give us the details on how you can balance the budget, Governor."

Focusing on the How introduces fear and doubt. If you work at thinking through the How, then you leave too much room for fear and despairing doubt to seep into your mind. Again, Nike's ad line is helpful: "Just do it." The How will show up at the proper time!

I guess it's about time to go on down the mountain and back out to building your dream. Remember, you need to come back here about once a week.

> *Having a strong and focused north star of purpose is more important than knowing HOW you're going to achieve that purpose. The "why" will give birth to the "how."*

Reading this book has been an exciting journey, hasn't it? The fact that you completed this book and have found – or are in the process of finding – your Why in life proves to me that you are destined for greatness.

I won't say that your journey to the full development and enjoyment of living your "Why" is going to be easy, but you hold a great key to success in this book. I don't say that because of my ego. I say it, because the truths in these pages are time-tested and proven to be effective. They worked for me, and they have worked for literally thousands of successful people.

In this book, you have been given an iron-clad blueprint that will guide you through the basics that you need to "Find Your Why and Fly!" You are a Champion so take time to "Find Your Why".

Always remember, my fellow Champions, that when THEY say there's no sense in going further and that everything has already been explored, don't believe it! Don't settle for mediocrity and being normal or average. Just keep listening for the sound of that little voice within that continues to tell you that it is possible. It still calls out just as strong and just as clear as it did to Thomas Edison, Andrew Carnegie, Napoleon Hill, George Washington Carver, Helen Keller and millions of other Champions throughout history.

That something hidden down deep inside is your "Why". It waits. Go and search for it. It is waiting for only you! When you find it, write and tell me about it. Send me a copy of your Why card. I want to hear YOUR story.

Oh, one final thing...

Don't forget to join the Motivational Club. We're all familiar with clubs. People have clubs for real estate, movie clubs, book clubs, knitting clubs, clubs for sports, etc., but how many of you have ever belonged to or even heard of a club devoted to building motivation for success? Imagine it...a club that only exists to help you find the right motivation and gives you the ability to join with Mastermind Team members that will support your dream and encourage you toward the fulfillment of your Why.

When you join, every month we will send YOU a motivational CD and a DVD, and you will also have access to prerecorded Monday

Night Millionaire Motivational LIVE Tele-Classes. Above and beyond that, there is an interactive Champions forum, where you can actively network and associate with Champions all over the world.

I believe this club is a MUST for dream builders. Start building your Mastermind Team today by visiting:
www.FindYourWhy.com/club.

Why Cards of Champions Just Like You

"My Why is I am spending time with Dennis; helping Philip with his College expenses and enjoying life. I am surrounded by children of all ages anxious for what they will learn today. My passion is to show and develop kids into seeing their own potential. Have a center where they can be surrounded by people that they can have on their own mastermind team. Sky's the Limit Youth Centers are all over the country giving our youth a positive place to explore the possibilities of their God given talents knowing that all things are possible as they put their trust in God's hands. The members of Sky's the Limit Youth Center, from the youth to adults volunteer at their local children's hospital helping bring joy and laughter to those who are not able to leave the hospital. I also give $20,000 on a monthly basis to Riley's Children Hospital. I am living on 25% of my income while the rest is used to support the Youth Center and helping children where there is a need. The best part of this is having my sons, Philip and Dennis, being a big part of the Youth Center. I am the champion that shows children they too can be a champion with unlimited potential.

- Loraine B., Indiana

"My Why is I am consistent in doing what I don't like to do and I watch my time like an eagle because I refuse to go with the flow of the masses due to the fact that I can clearly and precisely see and hear myself speaking and positively impacting grown adults, confused teenagers and creative children in order to illuminate the inspiring and hopeful stories of the bible that reveal The Truth, as well as stories of successful people in all walks of life who also went against the grain during their miraculous journeys. I will purchase at least one university campus with classroom buildings and dormitory rooms for 2,000 students, a 500-unit hotel in California and a 500-unit hotel in Florida for the International Youth Fellowship (IYF) and its expansion throughout the United States. My why is to have time, freedom and wealth so that the time God allows me to be on this earth will be spent with my family and the IYF, either traveling or enjoying heart-to-heart fellowship with each other as my life will be a testimony of The Living God as Jesus becomes greater and I become lesser."

– David R., California

"My Why is to create positive and rewarding change in my life. I am overcoming my adversities of fear and procrastination and accept the challenges I will face to have a return larger than life. I use my gifts to change peoples lives, giving hope to those who have none through inner peace and true happiness. I use my energy to provide my children with the opportunities they deserve by having old credit card debt paid by March 2006. I work with God, my family, and my mentor peers to succeed in my vision of prosperity. My relationships with God, myself, my family, and others that are motivated and committed to their purpose grow daily. As I fulfill God's plan for me, I accept the challenges, miracles, and unknown with faith, trust, and perseverance.

I have made the decision to reprogram using books, CDs, and seminars to fulfill my Why. With the power of God's Spirit working in me, I believe in health, wealth, success and action."

- Beth B., Georgia

"The reason why I'm dealing with all these challenges is for my own personal growth. Growth that covers many, many different areas of my life. Now I will allow myself to become who I was meant to become. I am making a difference today as a profit producing, fear demolishing, record breaker and an eye opening champion! I have my own direction now and was able to pay the mortgage off completely on our first home within three years of seriously, consistently working my network marketing business. I'm focused, organized, and actively engaged in building my business everyday. The income created from knowing all aspects of my business backwards and forwards, seriously wanting to get to know and care about others, while knowing the correct words to say to them allows me to tithe to my church and give donations to my many varied charitable interests. It's been a joy to know that the church's entire mortgage balance has now been paid in full.

I've specifically set aside the funds Marty needs to develop new churches to spread the Gospel wide and far. Having set up endowments for my nieces and nephews: Ceara, Keenan, Genesis, Kyle, and Lenaya, ensures that their college tuitions will be paid in full and they can have the funds they'll need to get a good education at the college of their choice while creating the foundation for their own future – or who knows, maybe even starting their own businesses as entrepreneurs. Crystal and Leadra won't have to worry about how pay their children's education. I'm building and living my own legacy so that I'll know I've made a difference in the world by becoming the best person I could be and accomplishing His plan for my life.

Through the foundation I've now established, I've been able to create a place where women who are victims of abuse can go and feel safe and not alone. Now they have a place where they can take the time needed to learn how to direct their lives in a positive way. Everyday, I see myself creating and expanding a circle that goes round and round and allows me to give back as well as receive unconditionally. This circle includes the phenomenal personal growth that will allow me to help other people who want more out of life become who they were meant to become.

I actually do see myself creating the financial independence for me and my husband that allows us to do what we want to do with who we want to do it. We travel whenever we want to - First Class Always! I love visiting cousin Amos in Mexico who always treats us like royalty when we come to see him. And I love our two homes: The condo off Lake Shore Drive on the top floor of Lake Point Towers in Chicago - especially since I've always wanted to live there ever since it was first built when I was just entering high school. I so enjoy watching the sun rise in the east out on Lake Michigan while sitting in my living room with its floor to ceiling picture windows. And I enjoy just as much watching the sunset while sitting on my balcony outside our extremely large master bedroom suite at our mountain condo in Beaver Creek

Colorado; that's where I first learned to ski. Now we're looking for a place where we can enjoy the ocean. (Mexico or Florida – maybe both!)

It's so comforting to know that as we get older, I'll never have to worry about medicare costs or nursing home expenses because I've created the residual income to cover anything we'll need to live comfortably and be well taken care of. – both of us. All through the vehicle of network marketing!

And to know that when I pass over I can stand before Jesus, who've I accepted as my Savior because he died on the cross for my sins, and hear the words I want so much to hear ... "I've been waiting for you. Welcome to your new home in heaven for all eternity, well done my child! ...brings tears of happiness to my eyes, even as I write these words, from just thinking about it. WHAT AN INCREDIBLE JOURNEY - WHAT AN INCREDIBLE BLESSING! And all because I choose to daily step out on faith and CLAIM MY DESTINY!"

– *Geri W., Illinois*

"My Why is to see my girls having a life full of love, joy and happiness. I will be a role model to nurture their hearts, mind and spirit and to help them be wholly who GOD made them too be. I see myself spending more time with them and my wonderful husband. I see us debt free and overflowing so that I can support causes that I believe in like Mercy ministries and a children's mission that gives orphans a safe secure home, love and care, an education and skills to move on in life. I will fund the protection of gorillas, because I am passionate about them. I also see us having the other half of our house built and have a walk in wardrobe with a place especially for my hundreds of pairs of shoes. I see myself traveling the world and going to places that before were only in my dreams. I see myself visiting Hillsong church in Australia and going on romantic trips with my husband. I am going to design and do photography. I will also have an outstanding, sporty car."

- Nancy G., United Kingdom

"I am diligently building my business today by sharing the gift of hope, health, and opportunity by doing all I can to become all I can and giving all the glory to God. I am changing the lives of a million people worldwide through personally enrolling one thousand associates that share my vision for total financial freedom and want to make a difference. As I do this, I am a loving and caring husband and father. I am enjoying an abundant lifestyle and am building a lasting inheritance for my children and my grandchildren. I tithe to my church, donate to Acts One Eight and MannaRelief Ministries. I am a blessing to others. Today, I am making a difference."

– Michael P., United Kingdom

Learn more about John's commitment to creating 1,000 Millionaires by visiting
www.FindYourWhy.com

"I am dealing with the challenges of building my business today because MY Why is to spend more quality time with my family, provide for my children's education, and have the finances needed to take regular family vacations and be a mentor to my kids. I will be in a financial position to finance my son Edward's dreams to become a pilot. By the year 2011, my monthly check will be at least LM 100,000, and I will be a Millionaire. I will tithe 10% to charitable institutes of my choice. I will open a special sailing training school with facilities for children with special needs so that they can enjoy the sport of sailing. I will have time to practice my pastimes such as sailing and trekking. I will own a luxurious 50ft sailing yacht.

I will own a warm, luxurious home with a pool that will be surrounded with plenty of land. I will own property abroad. I am surrounded by joyous, happy friends. I will be on stage presenting with John Di Lemme. I will find ways to better the present education system, and people will want to listen to me. I am making a difference today as a profit producing, fear demolishing, record breaking, mind blowing and eye opening champion."

- Kenneth T., Malta

"My Why is to allow a divine dream to be manifested through me. I will step into the fullness of my life purpose. I will use my gifts to inspire, empower and encourage 100,000 people worldwide to develop their gifts, fulfill their life purpose and be used as transformation agents. I will assist in shifting the balance of human consciousness from poverty to prosperity, from oppression to liberation, from fear to faith, from greed to generosity, from bitterness to forgiveness, from violence to peace and from hatred to love. I will be remembered as a woman that set the world on fire with love."

– Jasmine S., United Kingdom

"By 2008, I will be making $20,000.00 per month. Ken and I are going to build a new ranch style home with a two-car garage, an indoor swimming pool, and 5 bedrooms. Three bedrooms will be specifically decorated for my grandchildren to suit them in gender and age. Dustin will be 17, Ashley will be 15 and Zachary will be 13. There will be a personal bathroom off of each bedroom. Ashley's room will be pink and white with a canopy bed, matching dressers and a glass door hutch for all her dolls. Dustin's room will be timber green baseboards and wood paneling because he is older. Zachary's room will be blue with smoked grey window trim and baseboards and his choice of a bed and dresser style. The walls in Dustin, Ashley and Zachary's rooms will be covered with family pictures and their dreams in life.

The master bedroom will be in black and red, with a bathroom that has a Jacuzzi, a sauna, and a tanning room. Game rooms will be equipped with all the toys and electronics Dustin, Ashley and Zachary can enjoy that my daughters can't afford to give them. On weekends and holidays, they will have their very own retreat when visiting with Nana. The front yard will have a garden surrounding the entire front of my house and a gazebo in the back yard to accommodate fifty people for special events. My time will be utilized everyday building my business therefore, my yard will be kept up by a gardener.

I am going to donate 10% of my monthly earnings to help establishing programs for children with ADHD. It is my goal to see changes made for the parents and children of these families so that they can all learn how to cope with every day life and medicine free. Another 10% of my monthly earnings will be donated to the aid of exploited children. They are the wave of our future.

In 2011, my life as a millionaire will be set in motion and then I will be on my way to bigger and better dreams, because no one should ever stop dreaming."

– *Thelma M., Canada*

"My Why is to provide financial freedom for myself and my family so that Bob and I can travel the world, teaching and speaking at events all around the world and making the most of every opportunity that presents itself along the journey. I will donate at least 10% of my income to charities that are working to educate the very poor and disadvantaged in every society so that they can break the cycle of poverty and ignorance. I will also do volunteer work where I can help the most with the skills I have developed. I will educate my family and friends about how to secure their financial future, and then introduce this same knowledge into schools especially high schools so that children will realize that they have options other than further schooling to achieve their dreams. I will form a fund-raising foundation – 'Spirit Hug' – to assist, teach and nurture anyone whose spirit has been damaged or broken, regardless of age, race, location or faith so that they realize they are of value and are loved. I will become the person I know I can be, the person who is achieving these goals and using all of my creative abilities, living and loving with passion, and radiating joy."

– *Leanne W., Australia*

"My Why is to become financially free so that I can share the keys to my freedom with others. This will enable me and others to live a life of destiny and embark on the journey of desire. I will be a motivational speaker and will empower people to take control of their lives and develop the skills necessary to live the abundant life that God has got planned for each one of us. I will speak with the great John Di Lemme at an international convention. I will build the other half of my house for my family and friends to come and know that they are safe and loved. I will empower those same friends and family members to join me on the road to freedom. I will enjoy love, unity and excitement with my beautiful wife, Nancy, as we realize our dreams and empower our children to live their dreams."

– *Barrie G., United Kingdom*

Learn more about John's commitment to creating 1,000 Millionaires by visiting
www.FindYourWhy.com

"My WHY is to give my daughters everything that I can. I want to drive them to school in the morning and sing songs in the minivan on the way to school while looking in the rear view mirror at God's most beautiful creation. In the summertime, we're going on family vacations and staying at the best resorts. When I become really wealthy, I will give my wife thousands of dollars and make her spend it all on a shopping spree. She worries so much about our finances so I never want her to have another sleepless night. Lastly, I will be presenting a check for $100,000 to Montgomery Community Church. It will be at the 10am service and Pastor Tom will never see it coming. I accepted Jesus Christ as his savior this summer and want to shower my favorite church with money and let them distribute it however they see fit.

This is my WHY! I've had to stop typing several times to wipe the tears from my eyes. I have a dam of emotion built up inside of me. I have a commitment level that is off the charts. My energy has never been higher. When I was a kid I stuttered so badly I hung up the phone on my friends when they answered because I couldn't say their name. Now you can't shut me up. I'm telling everyone how my life has changed. My book will be published and my speaking engagements will fill up in the next year. My success is imminent. It's not a matter of if, but a matter of when. I know the only quality day for my family right now is Saturday because I work all week and worry about work on Sunday. Everyday will soon be like Saturday."

- Sam C., Ohio

"I am an outstanding teacher, encourager and mentor to others. I help others massively to live wise, fulfilled and prosperous lives. I am changing lives and nations to the Glory of God!

I am Platinum Presidential, a millionaire and exceedingly prosperous in every area of my life. My business extends into many countries, and I have developed some fantastic recruiting and training tools that strengthens my team and gives me another income stream. I have bought homes in the United States and Europe. I am abundantly blessed to be a blessing and extremely generous to the poor. I am featured on TV and radio talking about my projects and activities.

I have set up 100 orphanages in at least 5 different third world countries. I fly in my beautiful private jet with my team at least every few months to visit our homes and orphans. We are delivering life giving Glyconutrients, teaching materials and other necessities. We educate the children in health, and they receive education at the schools we have built and massive personal development ...they know there why and will fly. The children love God, worship and pray for nations. As we preach to the local areas, we see miracles, signs and wonders.

I am very healthy, strong and energetic; my youth is renewed like the eagles as I wait upon God. I am married to my soul mate. We have an outstanding relationship and are true partners in business and mission. Our children reflect our passion for God and are like arrows! Our household is flourishing in every way. We are able to leave a huge inheritance to our children and to our children's children. I serve, obey and follow God, he gives me uncommon wisdom, understanding, prosperity, fun and adventure!"

– *Emma P, United Kingdom*

Young Champion Why Cards

"I will show people how exciting, fun, adventurous, happy and beautiful that I am inside and out. I will travel the world and help children. I will have a wonderful house and family. I will share all of my thoughts and dreams with someone, and I will show them how much I have to offer as a partner, a mother, a friend, and a woman. I will prosper in my life and be debt free. I will be fit and healthy. I am not afraid. I am confident. I am living everyday to the fullest. I am sharing my faith with others. I will shake John Di Lemme's hand. I will speak to women and empower them not to be afraid to be who they are. I will make them feel beautiful, special and unique. I am surrounded by real people that are not consumed in all their doom. I am full of life, love and joy. I will ski, hang-glide, skateboard, surf, skate, quadbike, snowboard, act and dance. I will lead a youth group. I will be an individual that people look up to and come to for advice. I am role model for other women."

- Lucy G., age 16

"My Why is to be a millionaire by age sixteen. I will achieve this by working hard at my website www.funrocks.biz and writing an e-book called "How an 11-year old kid got an internet business and how you can succeed too". I will give at least 10% to homeless people with kids, kids charities and the Heart and Stroke Foundation because my granddad had a stroke. I am a kind, giving person that plays baseball and golf all of the time. I will be a PGA professional golfer, build robots and take over my parent's business. I will have a nice family living in a big house with two kids and maybe a dog."

- Erik A., age 11

"My Why is to be free and rich. I want to have my own wildlife sanctuary without all the bars. I will have a big house with a garden. I will have my own art studio. I will live in a safe place. I want to be able to save other people's lives and let them be free. I will give money to charities and other causes. I will run marathons for charities. I want the world to be peaceful."

– Aimee H., age 9

"I will travel the world. I will look after baby monkeys. I will be a hairdresser. I will live in America. I will have a mansion with a massive back yard and a pool. I will have a hamster. I will swim with dolphins. I will do ballet. I will go surfing. I will have a silver convertible and a motor bike."

- Harriet G., age 8

Learn more about John's commitment to creating 1,000 Millionaires by visiting
www.FindYourWhy.com

"I will go round the world and live in America. I will surf and scuba dive. I will also swim with dolphins and baby sharks. I am going to be a dancer and singer. I own five horses with their own stables. I will go snowboarding. I am going to be rich and successful. I will own a Ferrari and a land rover. I will own big house with a plasma screen television and a dog. I will also handle gorillas."

– *Tilly G., age 10*

"My Why is for my family to be rich and healthy. I will be a professional gymnast. I will live in a big house with a swimming pool and have lots of fun things to do. I will also have a nice car that I can drive around in. I will have a big screen television in my bedroom. I will live near the sea and swim with the dolphins and touch a starfish. I will travel round the world to give people the Mannatech products and some Manna bears.

- *Demi S., age 8*

My Why Is...

_____

_____

_____

_____

_____

_____

_____

_____

_____

_____

_____

_____

_____

_____

_____

_____

_____

_____

_____

_____

_____

_____

JOHN DI LEMME'S
Weekly E-zine
www.FindYourWhy.com

Home | John's Story | Success Library | Motivational Club

LIVE Seminars | Personal Coaching | Tele Classes | Testimonials | Weekly E-zine | Wall of Fame | Team

JOHN DI LEMME
Strategic Business Coach

Find Your *Why* and *Fly*
FREE Weekly Ezine

Rated by Industry Experts
around the world
as one of the
Top 5 Personal Development
ezines on the internet today
for over 5 years.

Sign up now for John Di Lemme's

Daily Dose Motivational Updates, Cutting Edge News plus Tele Classes in the Success Arena

You will receive important and timely news and updates from John on the topics you want to know about as they happen.

This will keep you in the loop and ahead of the curve.

And you will receive special notices and freebies that I do not reveal to my 'once a week' subscribers.

You will also receive the 'once a week' Weekly Ezine from John summarizing the week.

Your email address will not be given out to anyone, it is only for our use in sending you our *Daily Dose* and update information.

Yes, John!

Please sign me up to receive the *Daily Dose* Updates and News, and thank you John.

All information must be included to process your email subscription.

Follow me to...
http://www.FindYourWhy.com/dailydose

You'll love the *Daily Dose*

Go for it...

Follow me to...
http://www.FindYourWhy.com/dailydose

Register for upcoming
Millionaire Academy Boot Camp
Call 1-888-656-2267.

The Worlds #1 Leading Authority in Personal Development, John Di Lemme Needs Your Success Story

FREE 30 MINUTE "UNLEASH YOUR FREEDOM" PHONE CONSULTATION

Fill out the form on the following page for your FREE 30 minute phone consultation with one of John Di Lemme's top coaches. ACT NOW to claim your one on one session with one of John Di Lemme's top coaches! *(Limited Time Offer)*

John and his team are looking for 1,000 people that are tired of being frustrated and want to unleash their personal and financial freedom from within. You need to begin writing your success story this year, and we want to teach you the secrets of success in all areas of your life.

Picture yourself standing in your dream home, you are financially free and can spend your time doing what you want when you want. Just imagine yourself with a millionaire mindset...there is no more procrastination, disorganization or inconsistency. This is your chance to have the world's most elite Personal Coaches, Mentors and Trainers assist you with fulfilling your Why and finally achieving Personal and Financial FREEDOM!

John Di Lemme's proven secrets and strategies have touched the lives of HUNDREDS OF THOUSANDS of people worldwide!

☑ Yes John! I WANT to become one of the 1,000 millionaires that will be produced through your coaching program! Sign me up to receive my absolutely FREE 30 minute unleash your freedom phone consultation with one of your hand picked success coaches. I understand that this consultation will help me get clear on my network marketing goals, stop fear from holding me back, and help me become financially free.

Name _____

_____

Email_____

_____

Telephone_____

_____

Best Times to Call (EST.)_____

**Call Toll Free (888) 656-2267
or Send an Email to:
FYWCoach@FindYourWhy.com**

Mail Your Assessment to:
Di Lemme Development Group, Inc.
15104 Glenmoor Drive
West Palm Beach, Florida 33409

Send Your Assessment by Fax to: 561-687-8606

Life-Changing Ultimate Success Factor Bonuses

1. John Di Lemme's Top Ten Movies
   http://www.FindYourWhy.com/movies

2. John Di Lemme's Top Ten Books
   http://www.FindYourWhy.com/books

3. MLM Myths that are Costing You Millions – Finally Exposed!
   http://www.FindYourWhy.com/3myths

4. 8 Fundamentals that will Explode Your Network Marketing Business
   http://www.FindYourWhy.com/8fundamentals

5. The World Famous Monday Night Millionaire LIVE Motivational
   Tele-Class at 8:30pm EST – (212) 990-8000 – access code 7458#

6. The Eye Opening Story about Slavery
   http://www.FindYourWhy.com/freedom

7. The Startling News about 10,000 Baby Boomers Turning 50 Per Day
   http://www.FindYourWhy.com/boomers

8. 10 Tips to Make 2006 Your Best Year Ever
   http://www.FindYourWhy.com/10tips

9. Why Home-Based Business?
   http://www.FindYourWhy.com/homebusiness

10. M.L.M. Millionaire Academy Boot Camp No Joke Video
    Turn Up Your Speakers
    http://www.FindYourWhy.com/demovideo.htm

5 Millionaire Videos
(without the rental fee)

Millionaire Secret Video #1
Hear How a 24 Year Old Girl Closed Me
(and I'm glad that she did)
http://www.FindYourWhy.com/mentor

Millionaire Secret Video #2
Learn How a Canadian Housewife Now Earns More
Money Per Year Than 98% of Fortune 100 CEOs
http://www.FindYourWhy.com/karen.htm

Millionaire Secret Video #3
URGENT Success Reality - Unless You Decide to Grow
Everyday You Are Dead
http://www.FindYourWhy.com/resources

Millionaire Secret Video #4
How a Doctor is Breaking Records by Going Against
What Everyone Else is Doing
http://www.FindYourWhy.com/doctor

Millionaire Secret Video #5
MLM Millionaire Academy Boot Camp No Joke Video
http://www.FindYourWhy.com/demovideo.htm

About the Author

John Di Lemme was introduced to the industry of personal development in March 1990. John personally built organizations of over twenty-five thousand people in ten countries and retired to South Florida at the age of twenty-nine.

As the world's leading authority on personal development, John's personal coaching has assisted hundreds in achieving success and financial freedom. As a result of his experiences, John discovered that his personal passion in life is assisting others with believing in themselves and understanding that they truly can fulfill their dreams in life.

Now, John shares all that he has learned as a result of his hardships, challenges and successes. His trainings are full of inspirational and motivational true stories that are the basis of life. John's strategies have assisted thousands in moving to the next level of their lives and careers. His personal mission is to create one thousand millionaires worldwide.

Learn more about John's commitment to creating one thousand millionaires by visiting: www.FindYourWhy.com